Psychobiological Aspects
of Cognitive Growth

Psychobiological Aspects of Cognitive Growth

Reuven Kohen-Raz

School of Education
The Hebrew University of Jerusalem
Jerusalem, Israel

ACADEMIC PRESS   NEW YORK   SAN FRANCISCO   LONDON   1977

A Subsidiary of Harcourt Brace Jovanovich, Publishers

ACADEMIC PRESS, INC.
111 Fifth Avenue, New York, New York 10003

United Kingdom Edition published by
ACADEMIC PRESS, INC. (LONDON) LTD.
24/28 Oval Road, London NW1

Library of Congress Cataloging in Publication Data

Kohen-Raz, Reuven.
    Psychobiological aspects of cognitive growth.

    Bibliography: p.
    1.   Cognition in children.   2.   Psychobiology   I.   Ti-
tle.
BF723.C5K65   155.4′13   77-24343
ISBN 0–12–418050–7

PRINTED IN THE UNITED STATES OF AMERICA

*To Our Children
Noa, Achi, and Odea*

Contents

Preface

This book attempts to elucidate psychobiological aspects of cognitive development, but does not attempt to deal with the problem of causal linkages between biological and cognitive processes, which despite recent advances in genetics, brain physiology, and developmental neurology, are still largely unknown. The goals of this book are limited to a description of what may be defined as "borderline" phenomena of cognitive development. These are phenomena that can be observed and measured behaviorally, and also can be conveniently investigated by neurophysiological, genetic, and biological methods. Examples of such phenomena are relationships between physical and mental growth spurts; the interactions among complex motor responses that are accessible to neurological and psychological measurements; linkages between static balance ability and school readiness; the structure of the nervous system as related to symbol formation; the impact of physiological and mental processes on sensoritonic equilibrium; and seasonal effects on mental growth. By discussing such phenomena and the various efforts within various disciplines to investigate them, it is hoped that the common ground for interdisciplinary research and service in developmental psychology, education, and pediatrics will widen.

To a certain extent, this book also attempts to counterbalance the current overemphasis on the process of socialization as the central factor shaping the child's personality and intellect. Although it would be clearly mistaken to underestimate the major impact of social agents and institutions on human growth, psychobiological aspects of human development, consistently observed as indisputable facts but not always recognized to be important, should be given due attention when elucidating the etiology of educational and psychological problems in children and youth.

Educators (and possibly also psychologists) seem to abhor the idea of genetic, biological, constitutional, or neurological determination of behavioral phenomena in children, perhaps because they fallaciously assume that such physiologically determined behavior patterns are irreversible, thus limiting or precluding pedagogical intervention. Such educational pessimism seems not to be justified. Environmental, purely psychological traumatization may lead to firmly entrenched mental disturbances, whereas many of the effects of organic damage can be abated through educational measures, and many of the effects of genetically or constitutionally determined deficiencies can be counteracted by proper remedial measures. In fact, it may often be a great relief for parents to be informed that some minor neurological impairment—not their personal inadequacy—is the main cause of their child's educational handicap.

Another reason for the relative lack of interest in the role of psychobiological processes in education is the notion that many past studies concluded with weak or negative results concerning the relationship between physical and mental functions, and consequently seemed not to be worthwhile. However, closer inspection of these negative results reveals that, in most cases, an *overall* valid relationship was sought between the bodily function and its assumed mental correlate, without taking into consideration that such linkages are eventually limited to the duration of a certain *critical period*. In other words, it seems that psychobiological interrelationships are, by their very nature, *stage specific*. They may appear and reappear temporarily during development and can be entirely absent during long stretches of physical and psychological growth. Thus, unless one takes into account "critical stages of development" as appropriate frames of reference, potential effects of psychobiological factors on the educational process may remain unnoticed, and it may be erroneously concluded that they do not exist.

Having thus sketched the major objectives of this book, its structure will be outlined briefly: Following a review of "basic approaches" to the problems of psychobiological interaction in cognitive processes, some major theoretical contributions of prominent authors to this subject are presented, namely, Werner's sensoritonic theory, Rothschild's model of the biosemiotic structure of the nervous system, and Piaget's psychobiological interpretations of intellectual growth. This is followed by a general discussion of psychobiological aspects of cognitive development in infancy, and a report on physical correlates of school readiness, including some investigations on relations between static balance ability and reading skill. After a presentation of findings and theoretical considerations related to effects of birth season on physical and mental growth, the final chapter summarizes three studies on the impact of physiological pubertal maturation on mental achievements at adolescence.

The variety of theoretical approaches and empirical findings discussed in these chapters still leaves us far from providing even the basis of a comprehensive theory on psychobiological correlates of cognitive growth. However, it is hoped that some fresh insight will be gained on basic issues in educational and developmental psychology by viewing them from a somewhat different angle, and focusing on *nonsocial* aspects of mental development.

1

Basic Approaches

Both historically and in the context of contemporary research, psychological theory, experimentation, and practice are based to a large extent on psychobiological approaches to human behavior.

The emergence of modern psychology as a separate science and the severance of its parental ties to philosophy were primarily the result of experimentation based on definitively psychobiological (then called *psychophysical*) methods of research. These were designed and developed by investigators who were either physicians, physicists, or physiologists (for example, Weber, Fechner, Helmholtz, and Hering) or else neuroanatomists (for example, Bell, Muller, Flourens, and Hall) who hoped to discover the structure and function of neurological response systems, believed to be the basic correlate of all psychological phenomena. Although at the time of their discovery the well-known laws of Weber and Fechner seemed a giant step toward explaining the linkage between body and mind, the hopes they aroused were not fulfilled.

All the great psychological schools that were established later attempted to set up psychobiological bases for their principles. Wundt's and Titchener's structuralism dealt with the bodily bases of perceiving, thinking, and imagery. James, Hoffding, Dewey, and Angell, representative of the "functionalistic" and "psychodynamic" approach, aligned psychology with biology by introducing biological paradigms of organismic and social adjustment and models of genetic behavioral development.

Behaviorism adhered strictly to a neurophysiological and psychobiological conceptualisation, considering sensory stimulation, central nervous control, neural organisation of responses, as well as arousal and reduction of physiologically generated drives as basic phenomena of behavior.

Gestalt psychology established the principle of "isomorphism," stating that the concrete order of subjective experiences reproduces the dynamic functional order of physiological brain processes, i.e., both mental and organismic functions are governed by identical laws of configuration and organization, known as "Gestalt principles."

Another important school of modern psychology, psychoanalysis, originated in the extrapolation and application of biological and physiological principles in the domain of psychological processes. By virtue of a bold psychobiological conceptual framework, psychoanalysis profoundly changed the psychological and anthropological approach to man and mankind.

The monumental counterpart of psychoanalysis in the area of child development, Piaget's theory of cognitive growth, explains mental maturation as a continuum of stages of *psychobiological* equilibrium between the environment and the organism, striving toward an increasingly complex organisation of mental activities. The latter enable man to interact with spatially and temporally distant objects and elements and to master situations never experienced and never to be experienced. Although Piaget seeks to explain the genesis of man's highest mental capacities—formal scientific reasoning within a framework of logistic terminology—the frame of reference of his concepts is biological. It seems not to be accidental that the two great pathmakers of modern developmental theory, Freud and Piaget, began their careers not as psychologists but as physician and zoologist.

Finally, it should be noted that Gesell, psychologist and pediatrician, substantially contributed to our knowledge of early development and demonstrated that the child cannot be evaluated without integrating physical and psychological aspects of growth.

Despite the psychobiological foundations of modern experimental, developmental, and clinical psychology, psychology, which occupies a position between biology and the social sciences has developed two fields of specialization lying between the two—*physiological* and *social* psychology. This split may have contributed to the fact that the chasm between mental and physical processes has not been bridged. After a century of extensive research activity, the body—mind interaction is still much of a riddle. It seems that the investigations of the physiological and biological roots of behavior were conducted in close connection with neurophysiology and neuroanatomy, but the exploration of external adaptation and psychosocial relationships concentrated on measurements of overt responses and disregarded internal organismic events that were not directly observable.

Psychoanalysis, which was bound to offer basic explanations of the linkage between psychobiological and emotional—social processes, focused on phenomenological observations of individual cases in the context of clinical treatment and until recently abstained from systematic psychobiological experimentation.

Essential strides toward solving the mind–body problem were made by new and original methodological approaches, such as Penfield's (1969) electrical stimulation of human brains *in vivo,* Sperry's meticulous differential analysis of lateralisation of spatial and speech functions in patients with split corpus callosum (Sperry, 1968) and various experiments based on induction of motivational and instinctual responses by implantation of micro-electrodes in the cerebrum. (See below, pp. 4, 11.)

In spite of these advances, medical, biological, and behavioral sciences have developed largely in independent and sometimes divergent directions during the past few decades. In each field, knowledge and sophistication have grown immensely, but there has been no commensurate increase in either interdisciplinary cross-fertilization or integration of scientific information and aims and methods.

Abundant relevant material has been published. Although they do not yet take the form of a comprehensive psychobiological theory, some basic approaches to psychobiological problems have crystallised. These approaches will now be briefly described.

The following description does not pretend to present a survey of the vast literature that has accumulated in each of the research areas indicated. Nor can it elaborate upon the many related issues. It is intended only to demonstrate the complexity of the problem and the many possible avenues of research and to provide a background to the theoretical and empirical material discussed in the following chapters.

PSYCHOPHYSICAL ANALOGY

The assumption of psychophysical analogy between brain and behavior is one of the oldest and best known attempts to explain the body–mind interaction, and a large body of research has grown out of it. In a broad sense, the extensive search for "localization" of emotional, perceptional, motor, and mental processes in certain areas, layers, systems, or formations of the brain is based on this approach. The "isomorphism" between neurological and behavioral configurations of events postulated by the Gestalt theory is another version of this concept.

Essentially, it has been possible to find definitive linkages between physiological processes located in certain brain areas and typical behavioral responses. Two basically different methods have been used for this purpose. One is exemplified by the methods of Penfield already mentioned. Penfield's subjects were fully conscious during electrical stimulation of their brains, and provided reports of the sensations they felt. In experimentation such as this, presence of experimentally induced electrical stimulations causes the presence of a typical psychological activity (Penfield, 1969). Animal experiments along similar lines have been carried out. These include Von Holst's and Von Saint Paul's electrically induced and reproduced instinctual responses and behavior patterns in chicken, as well as Olds's study on cerebral self-stimulation in rats (Von Host & Von Saint Paul, 1962; Olds, 1956).

On the other hand, experiments of extirpation, separation, or devitalization of brain tissues aim to demonstrate the *absence* of behavior caused by dysfunction, destruction, or disconnection of the assumed "corresponding" brain area. In a similar vein, the exploration of symptoms in brain damaged or neurologically impaired patients seems to indicate that the affected parts of the brain and concomitantly disturbed behavior are structurally and functionally related (Luria, 1973).

It should, however, be kept in mind that if the impairment of a certain part of the brain causes typical deficiencies in mental processes, it cannot be implicitly assumed that the latter are located or "produced" in these cerebral areas, i.e., if the *absence* of a certain mental function is repeatedly concurrent with the impairment of a certain neurophysiological center, this does not prove that unimpairment of the latter would guarantee the presence of the former. In other words, although experiments and observations based on neurological deficiencies may lead to the discovery of necessary but insufficient causes of behavioral syndromes, the latter may be based on a much wider network of neurological processes.

Actually, an observed integrated behavioral response may be the result of a well programmed, complex interaction of several nervous centers, controlled by "circuits" and "systems" that typically encompass different "levels" and "layers" of the central nervous apparatus (Fisher, 1964; French, 1957). These circuits and systems are not "located" in certain brain areas. They seem to function in alternative, redundant connective constellations, an observation that might explain how healthy parts of a brain "take over" the tasks of the "impaired" areas, a phenomenon difficult to explain by localization (Milner, 1967). It also seems that the patterns of interaction between various cerebral "subsystems" undergo typical developmental changes, so that brain infections and injuries have different consequences at different ages (Dinnage, 1970).

Psychobiological research on child development based on localisation theory has serious limitations. Experimental electrical brain stimulation in children seems to be not only technically difficult but also ethically dubious. The determination of typical brain injury symptoms and syndroms through the accumulation and analysis of individual pathologies is complicated by the fact that in the exploration of the relation between types of physiological and mental impairment in the developing child, chronological age must be controlled and the size of comparable groups available for systematic investigations is therefore drastically reduced. Because there are indications that ethnic differences in early patterns of brain maturation may exist (Pampiglione, 1971) and that cerebral growth may be impaired by sociocultural deprivation (Willerman, 1972), control of additional intervening variables is required. Finally, if there indeed are mental changes in "brain organization," and "central nervous system interaction," localization and delineation of cerebral correlates of child behavior in general and cognitive growth in particular will be a difficult task.

THE GENETIC APPROACH

The potential of genetic research to elucidate psychobiological aspects of cognitive growth is obvious. Four approaches to this problem area seem to have developed.

The first is represented by investigations concerning certain types of mental retardation produced primarily by recessive genes and chromosomal aberrations. All these generally severe disturbances of mental growth are accompanied by physical symptoms and defects that are often used as reliable diagnostic signs of these syndromes. Some examples are phenylketonuria, mongolism, Tay Sachs disease, amaurotic idiocy, and Kleinfelter's syndrome. It will be noted, however, that there is no information about the intrinsic relationship between the type of physical defect and the patterns of mental impairment. Nor can any conclusions be drawn as to the eventual linkage between a certain gene structure (known to be defective or aberrant in the case of pathology) and its role in normal cognitive development.

The second approach to exploring genetic influences on mental growth is based on the comparison of intellectual development among identical and fraternal twins and regular siblings, sometimes using differences in educational milieu as an additional independent variable. This approach has generated many studies which, except for confirming what was already known, namely, that genes alone do not determine intelligence, failed to provide any reliable results about the extent and pattern of genetic influence on mental growth.* (For reviews of these studies, see Sarason, 1959, p. 448; Mittler, 1971.) The results of one of the best known investigations in this area (Skeels & Harms, 1948; Skodak & Skeels, 1949) seem to indicate that although the genetic component in intellectual development can be demonstrated, the educational environment produces decisively greater impact. The reason for the weak results of many twin

---

*Various biometric methods have been developed to estimate the relationship between genetic and environmental effects, based on correlational analysis between relatives, elaboration of heredity—environment ratios, and comparisons of within- and between-family variances. Jinks and Fulker (1970) have presented a comprehensive survey of new biometric models and approaches and illustrated their applicability by analysis of data collected and elaborated by other investigators. Although the data they used were often inadequate, they were able to demonstrate the usefulness of biometric techniques to produce new information on gene action.

studies seems to be the use of IQ instead of specific cognitive functions in basic measures, as well as the failure to control intervening variables only recently discovered by modern genetics (Mittler, 1971).*

A third avenue of approach has been opened by efforts to determine the role of genetic factors in the etiology of "sociocultural retardation." Research in this area has been obscured by the association of "genetic influence" with "racial determinism," which is bound to create ethical and political controversy. Jensen (1969) carried out an extensive systematic investigation of the complex interaction between presumably inherited and environmentally induced factors of sociocultural deprivation and their role in the impairment of mental functioning. In populations of the lower socioeconomic strata, there seems to be little doubt that constitutional intellectual weakness and lack of adequate social stimulation produce a vicious circle of adverse interaction that involves psychological and biological pathogenic processes, as shown by Pasamanick, Knobloch, and Lilienfeld (1956) and more recently by Willerman (1972).

In this context we mention Jencks' apt presentation of the various social and educational implications of the nature–nurture issue as related to the heritability of intelligence (Jencks, 1972). He concludes that although genetic effects on measurable intelligence level are indisputable and cannot be simply negated by liberal, "antiracist" ideology, their role in shaping the career of an *individual* child is practically not predictable and therefore of little, if any educational relevance. Also, the "environmental" influence of family background, economic stress and ethnic origin on IQs are being grossly overestimated by the psychosocially minded educator. Actually factors of far greater importance than those disputed in the heredity–environment controversy should be considered, namely: (*a*) the influence of the genotype on environment, in that he provokes typical–favorable or unfavorable feedback from social agents, (*b*) The distribution of educational and economic "opportunities" as determined and manipulated by society, and (*c*) general changes in the style of life of societies and ethnic groups, produced by overall cultural, economic, and educational progress and enrichment during relatively short time spans.

An important question, not yet sufficiently explored, relates to developmental–longitudinal changes in genetic impact on intellectual performance. It is generally assumed that the impact of the environmental factors is cumulative and chances to change, revert, or compensate deficits caused by genetic or constitutional influence decrease with increasing age (Bloom, 1964; Deutsch, 1967). The validity of this assumption has by no means been firmly established, however,

---

*A nearly unique opportunity to control such variables in twin studies is offered by the Kibbutz, where the influence of educational processes can be manipulated while all other sociocultural factors are kept constant, in that experimental groups of twins can be raised apart in different children groups without being separated from their Kibbutz, homes, and parents. However, except for one study (Natan, 1970) no advantage has yet been taken of these circumstances.

and "delayed" effects of genetic, prenatal, and early postnatal factors seem to exist (see pp. 8, 68, 73).

Wilson's recent longitudinal twin studies shed new light on this issue. They have shown that there is a pronounced genetic impact not only on mental achievements but also on mental growth rhythm during infancy. Wilson also reports a fairly evident genetic influence on mental performance during the preschool years, with differential patterns between the sexes and definitive signs of "delayed genetic effects" in females older than three years and in fraternal twins at the time they begin school (Wilson, 1972, 1974). Later examinations of this twin population using the WIPPSI Scales has revealed genetic effects not only on the verbal and performance IQs but also on the differences between the two subscales and on the patterning of the 10 subtests of the Wechsler scales (Wilson, 1975). The author concludes "that within a broad range of home environment, the genetic blueprint makes a substantial contribution to cognitive patterning and development."

Long-term and persistent genetic influences on the noncognitive sphere were found in a sample of twin girls by Scarr-Salapatek (1969). Individual differences in social introversion–extroversion were highly heritable genetic factors accounting for more than 50% of the variance within families. Results also seem to indicate that this personality trait is shaped by continuous interaction between the environment and polygenetic inheritance, the latter remaining potent as age increases.

Genetic influence on behavioral measures of adaptability across settings (structured test taking versus free play) and across time (i.e., between age groups) were also demonstrated by Matheny and Dolan (1975) in the context of the Louisville twin study.

A fourth recent approach moves away from the restricted concept of a "nature–nurture" dichotomy. To replace the mechanistic model of cumulative environmental stimulation affecting a given predisposition of "inherited mental potential" a cybernetic paradigm is proposed, according to which genetic influence more resembles a control mechanism, operating according to predetermined computerlike programs. An important aspect of this concept is the assumption that an anticipation of "expectable" environmental factors is built into the genetic program because the latter cannot proceed normally without specific environmental stimulation at "critical" points of development.*

*This view has been exposed in different formulation by Scarr-Salapatek (1976) in the context of discussing the evolutionary perspective of infant intelligence. She considers

Canalisation to be a genetic predisposition for the development of a certain form of adaptation, guided along internally regulated lines. Environmental features are necessary for complete development or for the full expression of the adaptation, but the direction of the development is difficult to deflect. Environmental inputs that are necessary for canalized development to occur, must be universally available to the species, else this form of adaptation would not work [p. 173].

In other words, the genetic program to a certain extent seems to compel the organism to seek *actively* the appropriate stage-specific "stimulus diet" vital to the organism's natural growth. In the case of humans, this is predominantly provided by socialization and education. Consequently, there are no pure "genetically determined processes of mental maturation *per se,*" which scientists have tried in vain to isolate. It rather seems that genetically determined structures are like "do-it-yourself kits," delivered with minute instructions on how to assemble, activate, and operate the apparatus in order to become "functional." Loss of the "instruction manual" is no less fatal than loss of the parts or the user's inadequacy "to understand" instructions or "to handle the material."

This means essentially that besides the known mechanisms of genetic transmission of functional and structural deficiencies, growth disturbances might also be caused by disruption of the genetically programmed timetable of ontogenetic development or improper and insufficient social stimulation at critical periods of development.

According to this concept, genetic effects need not necessarily be most pronounced at the earliest stages of development. They may emerge at later phases, such as puberty. Their impact may also vary considerably according to the amount of "synchronization" of genetic and environmental effects, a concept coined by Lorenz (1960). It should, however, be borne in mind that in order to explore genetic impacts on cognitive development within such a conceptual frame of reference, subtler and more differentiated measures of various cognitive processes than those obtained by intelligence tests seem to be required. Mitler's and Bruner's recent approaches seem to be a definite move in this direction (Mitler, 1971; Bruner, 1972).

THE THEORY OF EARLY RESPONSE REPERTOIRES

The theory of early response repertoires (or inventories) is, to a certain extent, an attempt to link the genetic approaches outlined in the preceding section with learning theory (Staats, 1970).

According to this model, the organism acquires "hierarchies" of basic behavioral repertoires during earliest, and probably critical phases of its life. Although these behavioral repertoires may be based on genetically rooted "potentials" of skills and abilities, their range, level, quality, and strength are largely determined by what may be called early learning, through a primary, short, but very intensive interaction with the immediate environment. This brevity and intensity of acquisition might be caused by the great sensitivity of the newborn organism to specific stimuli. Such a view is presented by Moltz (1960) who explains "imprinting" in ducklings as rapid visual conditioning of the newly hatched bird, whose retina has been shown to be hypersensitive to moving stimuli.

According to the behavioral repertoire theory, such quickly learned responses, which are predominantly in the domain of neuro-vegetative and psychomotor processes, cluster and crystallize in the form of stable behavioral inventories and repertoires, which may erroneously appear to be "inborn" genetically or constitutionally determined abilities. These inventories represent nuclei around which more differentiated behavior gradually develops, obviously through much slower and less intensive learning.

The failure to establish these basic behavioral repertoires and hierarchies naturally leads to a "cumulative deficit" (Deutsch, 1967) in skills and abilities. As the individual develops, he may be labeled "mentally retarded" or "culturally deprived" because of assumed "constitutional" or "hereditary" defects. On the other hand, the infant "enriched" early will gradually accumulate increasing mental superiority by building up more and more effective and differentiated repertoires.

Staats (1970) presents the following examples of "basic behavioral repertoires" in infants and toddlers: "naming" or labeling objects, readiness to follow directions, the ability to control motor and affective responses through classical conditioning to verbal stimuli (which then gradually become internalized). In addition, Staats considers the "ability to learn"—which he assumes to be itself acquired by means of early and earliest interaction of the organism with an adequately stimulating environment—as another important repertoire.

Infantile autism (Kanner, 1972) seems to be a case in point. The "inborn" as opposed to "environmental" etiology is still in controversy. It might be aptly defined as a grave disturbance in the establishment and growth of "early response" inventories.

It will be noted that the concept of the basic behavioral repertoire is similar to Piaget's notion of "schemata." However, it seems that the theory of repertoires is most explicit in that focal behavioral inventories are defined exactly. The role of repertoire *hierarchies* is also emphasized. According to the concept, behavioral disturbances and cognitive retardation will be determined not only by defective structures, functions, or learning processes but also by the *location* of the deficit in the general hierarchy of repertoires. This interpretation does not follow Piaget. The theory of behavioral inventories also stresses a certain principle of "parsimony" in explaining "fixated," "hardly reversible," and idiosyncratic responses, potentials, and "predispositions." Such phenomena should not be attributed to biological and genetic factors unless it cannot be demonstrated that they can be attributed to early and earliest acquired repertoires.

Although the theory of early response inventories acquired during critical stages seems plausible, its systematic documentation is still poor. The crucial issue is the experimental investigation of "minute learning processes," which requires determining (*a*) their respective reinforcement gradients, (*b*) the critical frequency, intensity, and patterning of stimulation, and (*c*) the relative weight of what might be defined as primary "inborn structures" as opposed to the immediate impact of environmental stimulation and self-regulatory feedbacks. Important contributions in this area have been made recently by Bruner and his associates; these will be discussed in greater detail in Chapter 5.

THE INFORMATION THEORY MODEL

This approach, which is in part incorporated into the genetic and early inventory theories, tries to explain biological, neurophysiological, and behavioral processes on the basis of principles generated by information theory. Recent advances in biology have demonstrated that patterns of information processing in the cell nucleus are mediated by chemical transmitters. These discoveries have led to new interpretations of memory and seem to be leading to the detection of biological correlates of learning (Hyden, 1969). The laws of feedback loop and servomechanisms, borrowed from information theory, seem to be a better explanation of neurological control, coordination, and response mechanisms than the traditional "simple tracked" stimulus–response paradigm (Pribram, 1969). Information theory seems also to have stimulated interest in the processes of attention, orientation, and habituation, which lend themselves conveniently to interdisciplinary exploration from the point of view of both the neurophysiological and the behavioral sciences. The laws of optimal input, output load, and information complexity seem to be applicable to a broad spectrum of neurophysiological, perceptual, cognitive, and social interaction processes.

Piaget (1971), who has recently made wide application of cybernetic principles (see Chapter 2, pp. 19, 20), stresses the importance of cybernetics in explaining psychobiological aspects of cognitive development in that they provide valuable information as to the analogous patterns of interaction between the organism and its environment on cognitive and physiological levels.

The great advantage of the information theory approach is its promising multidisciplinary applicability. Traditionally, the use of cybernetic principles in both explorations of biological processes and research on cognitive development has been separate but concomitant. If continued along such lines, it might possibly lead to a cybernetic reformulation of ancient laws of "psychophysical parallelism." Therefore a certain reorientation of research efforts may be needed to focus on processes that could be simultaneously measured by neurophysiological and behavioristic methods, applying principles of information theory in both fields. Exact measurements of minute motor responses, such as eye movements, activity of muscles involved in speech, or body sway while maintaining static balance, may turn out to be fruitful avenues for systematic research in this direction. (See Chapter 6, pp. 60, 64.)

As will be seen later, there is actually no modern theory relevant to the exploration of psychobiological aspects of cognitive growth which would not use, to greater or lesser extent, the information theory model, including Piaget's recent reformulations of his theory of cognitive development in psychobiological terms (see Chapter 2).

THE ETHOLOGICAL APPROACH

Ethological research, based on meticulous observation of animal behavior in natural settings and systematic laboratory experiments, must be considered relevant to investigations of psychobiological aspects of cognitive growth, although its findings cannot be extrapolated and directly related to human psychology. The study of animal instincts offers broad opportunities to explore inherited, genetically determined forms of cognitive processes. Signal transmission and perception by animals and innate discrimination of stimulus configurations serve as "key stimuli" to trigger off instinctual response sequences. Furthermore, through comparison of the species-specific structure of organs, their functions and readiness to "expectable environmental stimuli," the interaction between biological and environmental determinants of adaptive behavior can be conveniently observed (Lorenz, 1960, 1970). When such observations permit an instinctive response to be defined and later evoked artifically by electrical or chemical stimulation of the brain, the cerebral centers controlling that behavior can be located (Von Holst & Von Saint Paul, 1962; Fischer, 1964). In a similar manner, the impact of hormones on instincts can be systematically explored (Levine, 1960).

Finally, the observation of the way in which social responses in animals are regulated by instinct mechanisms provides insight into the role of biological factors in social interaction and "social" intelligence (Eibl–Eibesfeldt, 1970; Guhl, 1956; Tinbergen, 1955). By its focus on the evolution of biologically determined behavior inventories, ethology implicitly takes into consideration their *developmental* aspects, so that findings are specifically relevant to psychobiological problems of growth and development. Recent attempts to explain certain features of motor and perceptual development in early infancy have assumed the existence of "innate response–readiness" schemata, a concept much closer to an ethological model than to classical learning theory (Bruner, 1972).

As discussed later (pp. 16, 17) Piaget's endeavor to elucidate the biological roots of cognitive growth leads him to refer systematically to ethological theory and findings. He considers instinctive response mechanisms in animals to be intermediate phenomena between the purely biological mode of adaptation and the skillful and "intelligent" behavior of anthropoids and man.

A contribution to the elucidation of biological correlates of cognition, based on ethological research and comparative anatomy, is Rothschild's theory of biosemiotics, described in detail in a separate chapter (Rothschild, 1962, 1963). The nervous system is seen as a multidimensional and multipurpose unit of subsystems that have certain specialized functions but act differently in different contexts depending on the situation confronting the organism. The anatomical structure of these subsystems, as well as their location in relation to the posture of the body in the context of the species-specific environment, are predisposed to serve the "existential needs" of the species optimally. Because these "existential needs" must be met by efficient communication between the organism and its environment, the architecture of the nervous system reflects the preferred communication patterns of the organism, determined by both genetically determined instincts and the impact of external stimulation. These communication patterns, comparable to those found in other communication systems such as language, can be said to obey syntactic and semantic laws, so that it seems justified to speak of biosemiotics. These laws of biosemiotics seem to explain the anatomical structure, functional hierarchy, and patterns of interaction between the brain and its subsystems and behavioral phenomena.

Not only does biosemiotic theory demonstrate that phylogenetically rooted interspecies differences in the structure of the nervous system reflect typical patterns of the organism's adaptation to its environment, it also throws light on possible ontogenetic stages in the function of the human nervous system related to mental development from infancy to adolescence, as will be discussed later (Chapter 4).

THE BIOCHEMICAL APPROACH

The biochemical approach attempts to elucidate the impact of metabolic and hormonal processes on brain functions, implicitly throwing light on possible linkages between biological and cognitive development. In this respect, several trends of research activity can be differentiated. The first, which will be of least concern here, is the great number of investigations of the relationship between hormonal changes and attitudes, which indirectly may influence cognition. It is assumed therefore that the hormonal shifts precipitated by puberty lead to alterations in interests and social perceptions (Jones & Bayley, 1950; Jones & Mussen, 1958; Faust, 1960). Another recent approach focuses on relations between hormones and social interaction (Leiderman, 1965).

As to possible effects of hormonal processes on cognitive growth, no direct evidence has been produced, although data on the relationship between maturation during puberty and cognitive development suggest that such effects may exist (Kohen-Raz, 1974).

Although it has been proved beyond doubt that metabolic and hormonal deficits and disturbances produce mental retardation (such as cretinism or phenylketonuria), research efforts to prevent or ameliorate states of mental deficiency by means of hormonal treatment have not yet yielded satisfactory results. Indirect treatment of metabolic disorders that threaten mental growth by means of dietary regime have been successful, as in the case of phenyl-ketonuria (Fuller, 1967).

Another area of investigation, based on a somewhat different methodology and pursuing predominantly pragmatic objectives, deals with the use of drugs as a means to improve learning ability in educationally handicapped pupils (Conners, 1970). It is generally believed that drugs do not have any direct impact on the impaired cognitive function but that they help to overcome states of hyperactivity, perceptual distractibility, and weak attention that are obviously an impediment to cognitive proficiency. There is still much controversy about the practicality, scope, and safety of drugs in special education, and there is still little information about the linkage between the biochemical process induced by drugs and the nature of the neurological function underlying the cognitive process that they are expected to alter.

Generally, it may be stated that although the biochemical approach is promising, there is still great need for systematic research in this area, especially with regard to child development. This is of peculiar importance because the prevailing half-truths, hit and miss experiments, and conflicting opinions of scientists are likely to create false expectations among educators and parents of mentally retarded and behaviorally disturbed children and lead to educational errors and failures.

ELECTROPHYSIOLOGICAL MEASUREMENT

Electrophysiological measurements embrace a variety of methods, of which the electroencephalogram (EEG) and electromyogram are the most relevant for explorations of psychobiological aspects of cognitive functions. One advantage of electrophysiological over biochemical methodology is the possibility of immediate and simultaneous measurement of the electronic components of the neurological process and their behavioral manifestation. Biochemical correlates of behavior can be assessed in the context of natural and spontaneous interaction of the organism with the environment, however, while electrophysiological measurement often requires artificial settings, sometimes involving immobilization, isolation, or induced sleep. This may cause serious limitations to development research carried out with children. For this reason, telemetric equipment, which enables electroencephalic measurements while the child is engaged in spontaneous activity, seems to be a prerequisite to the systematic investigation of electrophysiological correlates of cognitive functioning. This observation also applies to electromyographic studies, which seem to become increasingly important in the light of assumed linkages between motor and cognitive processes (see p. 65). It seems, however, that the fine muscular activity involved in speech and eye movements, proprioception of postural changes, or monitoring of minute diplacements is related to cognitive skills most closely (Edtfeld, 1959;

Kohen-Raz, 1970; Rey, 1969) and depends heavily on the efficiency of the gamma efferent system (Bergmans & Grilner, 1969; Granit, 1968). Electromyography of such processes seems to be delicate and difficult.

As for the contribution of EEG research to the understanding of cognitive development, besides the present scarcity of studies based on telemetric measurements, there are still considerable difficulties with the availability of normative developmental data to use as reliable correlates of mental scores.*

Attention has also been given to the possibility that ethnic factors affect cerebral maturation and the evolution of EEG features in young children, which would complicate the standardization of developmental EEG measures (Pampiglione, 1971).

Among the EEC variables selected as possible correlates of mental functions, the so-called "evoked potential" has shown to differentiate between subjects of varying intellectual level and cognitive ability (Ertl, 1969). However, in light of the results of a recent large-scale investigation of this subject, serious doubts about the relationship between intelligence and the evoked potential have arisen (Davis, 1971).

Nevertheless, important aspects of possible psychophysical relationships between cognitive functions and EEG patterns have been discovered by Karmel (1974). He has demonstrated that the positive component peak in evoked potentials is affected by the density of the contours of checkerboard-like stimuli presented to infants, the relations taking the form of U-shaped functions. He has also shown that the maximum amplitude shifts toward stimuli of greater contour density as chronological and neurological age increase. (See p. 50.)

Despite the present shortcomings of EEG research, it deserves to be considered a prominent and promising approach to the exploration of psychobiological roots of cognition and their developmental patterns.

Overlooking the variety of approaches to problems of interaction between physiological and cognitive development, the quality and quantity of contributions made by contemporary research in the behavioral and natural sciences is impressive. The fact that so many questions are still left open is less due to the lack of relevant information available in the specific areas of investigations, than to the inadequate and restricted communication and coordination between fields of specialization. Also, methods and approaches that have been successful with adults need to be modified for use with children and adolescents, and efforts in this direction often have been neither satisfactory nor consistent. Hopefully, these shortcomings will be overcome in the not too distant future.

*Such data have been provided by Henry (1944) and by Corbin and Bickford (1955). For general studies on the relationship between EEG and intelligence, see Knott and Friedman (1942), Kreezer and Smith (1950), Mundy-Castle (1958), Gastaut (1960), and Giannitrapani (1969).

2

Psychobiological Aspects of Piaget's Theory

Despite the impact of Piaget's work on teaching and research in cognitive development, the psychobiological basis of his theory is not duly recognized and appreciated.

Even without an analysis of the elaborate framework of Piaget's psychobiological concept of human intellectual development, a superficial examination of his vocabulary reveals that he makes extensive use of biological terms. Besides such basic concepts as *assimilation, accommodation, adaptation,* cognitive processes are described as *reactions,* governed by laws of *circularity* and *equilibrization* in the sense of physiological homeostatis.

Titles of his books include such terms as *growth* and *birth* (*naissance*) of intelligence, and the biological paradigm is easily recognizable in his references to phases, stages, and substages which interlink, interfere, crystallize, and stabilize as if they were biological phenomena.

It seems that Piaget's attempt to keep cognition within what he believes to be its natural organismic context is one of the sources of his elaborate and difficult style. It is likely that this attempt also accounts for the difficulties in "translating" his concepts into "familiar" behavioristic terminology. (On the other hand, it appears that behavioristic research, through its distance from biological concepts and its affiliation with psychophysical methodology, has encountered difficulties in interpreting and exploring developmental processes.)

Turning now from these impressions of Piaget's style of writing to its content, we realize that his concept of intelligence and its growth is truly organismic.

Intelligence, according to Piaget, is the highest and most flexible form of adaptation to an environment unlimited in space and time. Other forms of "organismic adaptation sensu strictu," typical of lower species and young infants, are based on reflexes as well as perceptual and sensorimotor responses.

Piaget (1976, p. 482) explains that the main function of instinct is to ensure the satisfaction of three basic needs—food acquisition, protection against foes, and reproduction. Perceptual and motor skills, as well as sensorimotor intelligence remain linked with these biological drives, whereas higher mental abilities (operational thought) transcend this functional frame, serving the needs to understand and to invent. Hence, the individual is able to relate to an extended milieu and to a universe of objects of knowledge.

It is thus Piaget's basic notion that all cognitive processes originally serve primary organismic needs, namely acquisition of food, protection against noxious stimuli, and reproduction. In the more primitive organism, the satisfaction of these needs is provided by the immediate, directly accessible environment. Therefore their cognitive activity is limited to sensation of nearby stimuli and control of immediate movements toward or from them. Further up the phyletic scale, more and more distant and less probable aspects of the environment become critical and eventually vital to survival. Not only do constant vigilance and response readiness have to be maintained, exploration for the sake of "gaining experience" also becomes imperative. New types of cognitive activity appear, not tied exclusively to the mechanisms of primary need satisfaction but leading to the formation of structures, to the establishment of mechanisms of memory storage and retrieval, and to the organization of flexible and adaptive "response inventories" characterized by an increasing ability to find alternatives and seek detours. For Piaget, the highest intellectual functions, "formal scientific thought" (formal reasoning), represent the most elaborate and flexible cognitive processes, transcending the temporal and spatial boundaries of individual experience and becoming increasingly independent of empirical content.

One of Piaget's arguments to demonstrate the "homology" of intelligence and the general processes of biological adaptation is his interpretation of animal instincts. Instincts are organismically determined and biologically rooted. They function to ensure survival and are genetically tuned to respond selectively to stimuli and events which are not always of high probability. Hence their affinity to primary, immediate need satisfaction on the one hand (the biological component), and differential sensitivity to the spatially and temporally distant environment on the other (the "cognitive" component, which may be viewed as a precursor of "intelligent" behavior) (Eibl–Eibesfeldt, 1970).

Piaget attempts to interpret the origin of intelligence as the outcome of a dissolution of the instinctive mechanisms and their subsequent reintegration on a higher functional level: He maintains that with the development of mental abilities in humans, certain components of instinct, that is, genetically predetermined release mechanisms, vanish, whereas others are maintained, namely the capacity to organize temporal sequences and to adjust to the press and stress of the environment. However, these latter processes instead of being programmed (as it is in the case of instinct) now become autoregulated, mobile, and flexible and result in a mental interplay of corrections, anticipations, and reversible representations of actions.

Another interesting aspect of instinct, highlighted by Lorenz (1969), is the linkage between the inherited form of organs and their inbuilt, "genetically programmed," species-specific function. That is to say, Lorenz assumes that in order to ensure optimal adaptation of the organism to its environment, a common genetic program generates the characteristic shape of both organ and its instinctive response inventory. This interpretation of the integration of structure and function in the organism may be extrapolated to a psychobiological concept of human intelligence, in that the latter would be based on both organs being specially structured to serve skilled adaptation (especially the muscle system involved in hand–eye coordination) and "functional rules" activating these organs. In humans, these functional rules are decisively shaped by sensorimotor learning, imitation, and socialization. Piaget concedes however, that a clear demonstration of "homology" between the inherited functions, organs, and adaptive mechanisms underlying individual behavior in animals and human higher mental functions is difficult. There is a fundamental difference between sensorimotor skills and mathematical–logical operations. That is to say, the latter lead to a necessarily true conclusion entirely independent of immediate circumstances whereas the former reach temporary equilibrium by an ad hoc solution relevant solely from the point of view of the organism's momentary constellation of needs and tensions.

Piaget finds the fundamental difference between biological and cognitive adaptation at its higher levels (formal, logical–mathematical reasoning) in the possibility of dissociating form from content in the latter: I.e., in reflexlike and physiological responses, form and content cannot be differentiated. As intelligence develops, form and content become differentiable: Whereas concrete operations are still partially tied to content, formal reasoning proceeds without any commitment to substance, sensorimotor experience, or physical need reduction.

Piaget's search for parallels between biological and intellectual processes is only one of his approaches to psychobiological aspects of cognitive growth. Another approach to this problem involves a comparative analysis of the evolution of biological and psychological theories of human development. This analysis is based on an interpretation of major trends in scientific thought and conceptualization in the natural sciences and psychology throughout the past three centuries.

Piaget aptly notes that human scientific thought in both philosophy and the natural sciences has undergone three, if not four, phases of development and that these phases can be traced in biology and psychology.

During the first, prescientific stage, it was believed that the interaction between organism and environment, between man and the universe, was preestablished by divine activity, ensuring harmonious unfolding and molding of life in all its varieties and levels, including man's spiritual existence. Within such a system of thought, biological and cognitive processes were thought to function in a predetermined manner, each within the realm of a teleologically fixed destination.

This doctrine, defined by Piaget as "preestablished harmony," views the human organism and human intelligence as subordinated to a perfectly constructed universe. Consequently, there is no room for evolution and development either phylogenetically or ontogenetically. Nor is there any concept of biological and cognitive growth as gradual processes, composed of alternating phases of tension, disequilibrium, and reequilibrization. Piaget emphasizes that theories of preestablished harmony are not limited to the Aristotelian or medieval periods but can be found in more modern views of vitalism and finalism, in both biology and psychology, and in the nineteenth-century psychological approaches that attempted to explore and categorize "the faculties of mind."

The second phase is characterized by the "organism versus milieu," "heredity versus environment," "nativism versus empiricism" controversy. This controversy had a powerful parallel on theory construction and experimentation in biology and psychology.

Empiricism is represented, according to Piaget's view, by Lamarckism. Piaget remarks that:

> Lamarck is essentially a functionalist, and the accent put by his doctrine on the exclusively formative role of the environment evokes closely (the association) of empiristic epistemologies. The two central ideas of Lamarckism are the role of exercise of organs during the individual development and the hereditary fixation of the modifications obtained by this way (heredity of acquisition) [p. 151].

In the cognitive sphere, Piaget easily finds parallel theoretical models:

> If we think about a possible parallelism with relations between subject and object within the cognitive functional area, analogies emerge most strikingly. The doctrine, according to which the subject is wholly exposed to the forces of the object is *empiricism* in its classical form, for which the most fundamental concepts of reason were only due to repetitive effects of experience and to habits acquired by the subject under the pressure of circumstances [p. 158].

On the other hand *nativism* in biology has found its expression in the theory of mutation, which emphasizes that variability in the organism's shape, form, and characteristics is chiefly caused by alterations within the structure of the genome. The impact of the environment, besides "naturally" selecting the viable genotypes, is restricted to producing adaptive changes in the phenotype only. In Piaget's own words

> With the rediscovery of the Mendelian Laws and the discovery of mutations, a neo-Darwinism or mutationism, which we call "classic" in contrast to its actual considerable transformations, has eliminated from its doctrine every trace of Lamarckism, in order to put the accent exclusively on endogenic variations. Only the variations of internal origin (the so called mutations) are hereditary, being produced within the frame of the genotype, which by itself is considered by be invariant. The environment intervenes only post factum, by selecting the variations which have been produced in such way. (Without speaking about phenotypical variations, which are due to the milieu, but are of no evolutionary importance, because not being hereditary) [p. 162].

In the realm of psychology, Piaget considers Lorenz's theory of instincts, based (according to Piaget) on Kant's a priorism, to be the most prominent representation of the nativistic approach (1971, p. 168). Also Gestalt theory, in light of Piaget's earlier criticism, deserves to be called a nativistic model in the context of this analysis of biological, philosophical, and psychological trends and schools.*

Actually, psychoanalysis, apparently overlooked by Piaget, has certain "nativistic" trends, such as Freud's differentiation between "life" and "death" instincts, based on Weismann's dichotomy of germ versus soma-plasma, as well as his theory of the phylogenetic origin of the Oedipus complex (Freud, 1968a,b).

The closest parallel between biological and psychological concepts of human development, and the one of most immediate importance, is manifest in the third phase of "evolution of scientific thought," which may be defined as *interactionism.* This modern approach is gaining increasing impact and has been influenced by cybernetic models. It not only uses the computer extensively as a simulator of mental processes but also applies the principles of programming and operating the computor as models of biological and psychological theory. Three cybernetic principles are relevant in this context: inbuilt control, feedback, and interaction, the last term referring in biology and psychology chiefly to the two-way flow of information between the organism and the environment.

In modern biology, various new discoveries have given considerable impetus to the development of interaction theories and a cybernetic interpretation of biological and biogenetic processes. First of all, substantial advance has been made in controlled experiments on hereditary transmission of ontogenetically acquired characteristics and skills. The genotype seems to manifest processes of adaptation and assimilation similar to those observable in the phenotype. Second, the impact of the environment on both phenotype and genotype is accompanied by a complementary process through which the genotype, through

*See Piaget's introduction to his *Psychology of Intelligence* (1951, p. 15).

the phenotype, actively selects whatever environmental stimulation will optimally match the genotypic "programs," or eventually be "expected" to induce
typical changes in genotypic structure. Thus there is a continuous, dynamic
interaction among genotype, phenotype, and environment—a concept that integrates Lamarckian, Mendelian, and Darwinian approaches within a cybernetic
frame of reference. Third, the dynamics of the "genetic pool" are considered
more and more important in explaining patterns of mutations, which are not
"accidental"—as traditional mutation theory assumed—but "purposeful." They
demonstrate definite patterns of adaptation, assimilation, and selective interaction—between the milieu and the population on the one hand, and within the
population and its individuals on the other. Both processes are apparently
governed by laws of self-regulation and feedback that involve changes on the
level of both genotype and phenotype (Dobzhansky, 1969). Fourth, the discovery of the differential role of "transmitter" and "regulatory" genes, the latter
being probably responsible for the programming of growth, the timing of its
developmental phases, and the sensitization of the nervous system to interact
with the "species-specific," "expectable" environment.

This contemporary biological model, replacing the antagonism between
Darwinism and Lamarckism with a cybernetically conceived, complex, and
multidimensional interaction system, seems to suit Piaget as a basis for reformu-
lating his own theory of cognitive development as a parallel solution to the
dilemma between a priorism and empiricism in the behavioral sciences. As
formulated by Piaget himself:

> The logical mathematical structures, are neither preformed, nor derived from objects,
> but require at the initial stages of their development a period of actions on objects of
> experience, during which they are indispensable. However these structures are neverthe-
> less not derived from the objects themselves, because they are constructed by means of
> operative elements, which are abstracted from the actions of the subject on the objects,
> as are the coordinations between these actions. We are thus confronted with an
> organisatory and regulatory functioning [of a cybernetic type]. A priorism was wrong in
> that it ignored that the construction [of these structures] cannot be realized without
> interaction between subject and objects, during which the latter constitute an op-
> portunity (incentive?), but not the cause (source?) of these formative regulations [p.
> 172].

To formulate Piaget's point of view in more general terms, it may be stated
that intelligence is eventually genotypically rooted, but not in the sense of a
"power" or "potential" determining levels or limits of adult IQ (as nativists in
the nature—nurture controversy would argue), but mainly in the sense of an
inherited sensitivity or "interaction readiness" of the organism and its "openness" to expand the range of such interaction. This "interaction readiness,"
described by some authors as "stimulus hunger" or "exploration drive," is
manifest in "circular reactions" characterized by active and repetitive search for

new stimuli and situations, which both enrich and stabilize newly acquired schemata by "assimilation," and render them more flexible by "accommodation." Piaget postulates a genotypically determined, active striving of the human mind to accomplish more and more differentiated and far-reaching interaction with the environment. This tendency is similar in principle to that observed among animals to search for stimulation and confrontation with the environment in order to attain mastery of activities related to primary needs.

Another "interactionist" aspect of Piaget's theory is the principle of "autoregulation" and "equilibrization." This principle is evident on both the biological and cognitive level. However, cognitive organization extends beyond vital organization and completes it where the biological level is insufficient to safeguard the survival and adaptation of the human organism.

Thus levels of intellectual growth in children are explained in terms of attaining a cognitive equilibrium. The child needs to come to terms with tasks, and the challenges of everyday life activate mental schemata adequate to the child's level of physical, emotional, and social development. As the child grows, the process of maturation, as well as social stimulation and changes in social expectation, cause "disturbance" of this equilibrium and lead to new forms of "mental homeostasis." These patterns are comparable to the structural changes that occur during biological growth, which—in the extreme form—are manifest in metamorphosis.

Such a psychobiological interpretation of intellectual development might prove to be helpful in defining differences among various types of retardation, in that they may be attributed to different forms of mental disequilibrium. That is to say, cultural retardation could be described as a typical lack of environmental challenge or stimulation to induce transition from lower to higher forms of mental equilibrium. Organic mental deficiency would be the result of externally inflicted damage to mental structures, and familial retardation could be defined as the result of insufficient inner tension or inadequate capacity for self-stimulation, possibly caused by minor defects in genetic programming.

A third aspect of the interaction principle represented in Piaget's theory is the recognition that society (at the level of intimate contact with caretakers and at the level of broader relationships with peers, educators, and social institutions in general) is a decisive regulatory and stimulative agent of intellectual growth. From a psychobiological point of view, this role is similar to that of the "genetic pool" which regulates the adjustment of individuals to the population, and the adjustment of the population as a whole to the ecological pressure of the environment by continuous feedback (Dobzhansky, 1967, 1969).

Piaget (1971) thus maintains, that

> Intelligence does not give up the transindividual cycles of instinct, but in order to entrust itself to interindividual or social interactions . In this respect, the social group

plays the same role from the cognitive point of view, as the "population" from the point of view of genetics, and consequently from the point of view of instinct. In this sense, society is the supreme unit and the individual does not achieve his inventions or intellectual constructions unless he becomes the seat of collective interactions, the level of which depends obviously on the society and its whole. In the area of cognition, the individual operations of intelligence and the operations which ensure exchange in cognitive cooperation are identical. The most general forms of thought, being dissociable from their content, are simultaneously forms of cognitive exchange or interindividual regulation, being at the same time derived from functions common to all living organisation [pp. 497–498].

To summarize Piaget's concept of the social function and social meaning of intelligence, it may be stated that a logically true consequence, reached by means of operational reasoning, either reflects or symbolizes an act that can be imitated and performed by every member of human society in exactly the same temporal sequence or spatial arrangement. Mental acts on the level of operational thought, when implemented in the form of a real task, thus guarantee perfect social collaboration. Consequently, higher level cognitive processes are the core of human social interaction, organization, and communication. The higher their level, the greater their power to engage human beings in tasks of mutual interest, to link spatially and temporally distant individuals, to master complex social situations, and to solve problems in a manner enduringly useful and beneficial to mankind.

Mature cognitive functions thus play an essential role in fostering the survival of humans as social beings. From this viewpoint, the psychosocial functions of the intellect serve the psychobiological needs of the human race to build and maintain the socially effective patterns of communication vital to human existence.

That by means of mental operations, man has supplemented his fragile organism with machinery in which he can fly to the moon is a dramatic demonstration of Piaget's thesis. The highest levels of cognitive processes are functionally equivalent to an expansion ad infinitum of the human organismic power of adaptation to environmental circumstances extremely remote from its original biological habitat.

On the other hand, regression to infantile, "preoperational" patterns of reasoning in social relationships between adult individuals and between groups or societies provokes social conflict and results in disruption of these groups, ultimately leading to the biological damage or destruction of their members.

Any attempt to evaluate Piaget's psychobiological interpretation and general theory of cognitive development would probably conclude that his major contribution has been the application of cybernetic principles to developmental research in general and to the exploration of genetic epistemology in particular. His postulation that the same laws of self-regulation and feedback govern both the patterns of interaction between genetically preprogrammed and environmentally "expectable" events, including molecular processes of "self-stimulation," establishes a common outlook on biological and cognitive growth. Traditional developmental psychology has remained fixed within a conceptual framework developed during the "technological era" and characterized by a focus on models of machine construction and the utilization of physical energy. It is noteworthy how many concepts taken from physics and reflecting aspects of energy regulation have become entrenched in psychological terminology: habit *strength, intensity* of drive, *latency* of *response, extinction, action* and *reaction,* response *mechanism, level* of adaptation, libidinal *energy,* ego *weakness* and *strength,* superego *pressure, suppressed* wishes, and psycho*dynamics.*

Such concepts, even if they are valid in the field of general psychology, become inadequate when they are used to explain developmental phenomena. In this respect, Piaget's psychobiological concept is definitely superior.

There can be little doubt that Piaget's theory, both in its general form and in its more explicit "biological" formulation (Piaget, 1971), is a major contribution to the elucidation of psychobiological aspects of cognitive development. He may be criticized, however, for not translating his theoretical framework into operative terminology which could be used in systematic empirical research designed to explore the relationship between neurophysiological and psychosocial factors of intellectual growth. Actually, Piaget himself introduces his book *Biology and Knowledge* (1971) as a "gathering of *interpretations* rather than of experimentation . . . [although based on] forty-five years in psychological experimentation in development [and] as full as possible acquaintance with the main currents of contemporary biology" [p. xi].

Still, Piaget's experiments, although they were carried out throughout five decades and although they fully took into account psychobiological and organismic aspects remain strictly in the realm of *behavioral* exploration from an operational point of view. Obviously, we would be interested to know the critical stages of cognitive growth during which the "genetic roots" of intelligence might be most affected by certain types of environmental factors. It would also be worthwhile to investigate the reversibility of the debilitating effects of endogenous, exogenous, or socially induced mental retardation. Another crucial issue would be the exploration of the duration and intensity of environmental stimulation, presumably needed to induce changes in the genotypical disposition of cognitive abilities. A list of research topics would surely include the following questions:

How can retarded cognitive growth be stimulated by drugs, and how can the drug effect be explained in the light of brain anatomy and cerebral neurophysiology? How does sociocultural neglect affect cognitive development, directly or indirectly, by impeding normal neurophysiological growth of the nervous system, etc.*

*Willerman (1972) has summarized important aspects of these problems.

It is also doubtful whether Piaget's biological interpretation of cognitive growth has succeeded in explaining and describing the emergence of higher cognitive functions, especially formal reasoning, in biological terms. In other words, can it be demonstrated that in humans sensorimotor mechanisms—originally used to satisfy biological drives and meet the stress of the immediate physical environment—develop continuously into patterns of mental interaction with real, imagined, or symbolized facts and data, transcending the limits of man's materialistic existence in time and space and essentially independent of his organismic needs? Can scientific thought really be defined as a psychological process, obeying the structural and functional laws of biological adaptation seen in the behavior of the human infant? Can it be proved that formal and abstract thinking is the highest form of the "typically human," species-specific way of equilibrization between an intrinsic, biologically rooted urge to explore the universe and a multidimensional social environment structured by complex symbol systems and shaped by cultural tradition? Finally, can it be shown experimentally that striving for such an "existential" equilibrium is determined by a genetic program based on biological laws and principles?

Faced with all these open questions and aware that many parts of Piaget's theory are still highly speculative, one must admit that he offers a comprehensive theoretical framework that may serve as a convenient and useful basis for future interdisciplinary research on psychobiological aspects of cognitive growth.

3

Sensoritonic Theory

Werner and Wapner's sensoritonic theory of perception, although originally designed to explore patterns of perceptual development, has contributed to the understanding of psychobiological aspects of cognitive growth. This is evident from the postulate of this theory that there is a continuous interaction between perceptual processes and the psychophysiological state of the organism. At every instant of organismic alertness, the preceptual receptivity and the psychomotor response readiness of the individual are determined and structured by flexible states of organismic tension described by the authors as "sensoritonic equilibrium" (Wapner & Werner, 1957).

This sensoritonic equilibrium regulates perceptual and sensorimotor processes by a principle of vicarious interdependence. Sensory input from various sources impinging upon the organism at every moment of its interaction with the environment produces disequilibrium which is counteracted from within by the organism's striving toward "sensoritonic equilibrization." This is achieved either by changes in the perceptual field leading to reorientation in space or by increase of muscular tension compensating the "field disturbance" or by overt motor activity or postural readjustment. All these alternative responses intended to prevent the organism from being overwhelmed by the stimulation.

According to sensoritonic theory, three kinds of stimulation, "object," "extraneous," and "introceptive," are to be differentiated. "Object stimulation" refers to the direct stimulation by the object on which the subject's attention is focused. "Extraneous stimulation" is caused by situationally proximal stimuli which often activate sense modalities different from those mediating "object stimulation" but decisively change the pattern of perceptual and motor responses evoked by the latter. Examples are the impact of body tilt upon the perception of the vertical, the effect of color or sound on the maintenance of body balance, the change of threshold in the perception of apparent movement produced by directional cues, and the influence of immobilization of the body on the production of "movement responses" in inkblot tests. In all these instances, body tilt, color, sound, immobilization, and directional cues would be considered sources of "extraneous stimulation." "Introceptive stimulation," finally, refers to proprioception of internal physiological states and muscular tensions. Sensoritonic theory further postulates the existence of "vicarious channelization" and "functional equivalence" between the psychological and physiological processes generated by either one of these modes of stimulation. As formulated by the authors themselves:

> It has been found empirically, that head tilt, body tilt, direct stimulation of neck muscle, auditory stimulation, rotary acceleration around the vertical axis of the body ... all function in an equivalent manner with respect to perception of verticality. ... Asymmetry in the terms of physical location (left or right of observer) and asymmetry in terms of arrangement of the parts of a configuration may affect the perceptual straight-ahead in an identical way [Wapner & Werner, 1957, p. 4].

An example is the vicarious influence of the tilt of a rod and the body tilt of the experimental subject on the perception of verticality. In this case, there is a compensatory equivalence between object stimulation and extraneous stimulation, i.e., tilt of the rod to the left or body tilt to the right both have the effect of shifting the apparent vertical counterclockwise. Another type of sensoritonic vicariousness is evident in experiments that elicit apparent movements by static stimuli. Here it has been shown that the restriction of overt motor responses vicariously increases the production of imaginary perceived motion described as "virtual movements" by Rothschild (1958) and Palagyi (1925). This vicarious movement perception can in turn be depressed by inducing another "secondary extraneous stimulus" such as color. An example is the reduction of vicariously produced movement responses to inkblots, when colored inkblots are presented instead of grey (Siipola & Taylor, 1952). It thus seems that the affective arousal evoked by color (secondary extraneous stimulation) offers an outlet to the sensoritonic tension created by movement restriction (primary extraneous stimulation) that originally would have been discharged through increased imagination of movements in static inkblots (object stimulation).

What are the contributions of sensoritonic theory to the explorations of psychobiological aspects of cognitive development? One major issue is the assumption that realistic adaptation to environmental stimulation is based on an organismic state of sensoritonic tension which may be also described as a state of response readiness or alertness. According to biosemiotic theory (to be discussed in Chapter 4), consciousness and, implicitly, clear differentiation between subject and object are induced by awareness of postural steadiness. This awareness provides what may be called a "proprioceptive background stimulation" against which extraceptive stimuli can be experienced as part of the "outer world," the "nonego." Obviously, the physiological antecedent of postural stability is optimal tonicity of the muscle system involved, which sensoritonic theory interprets as the proprioceptive component of the sensoritonic equilibrium. In this context, EEG studies have explored the relationship between diencephalic arousal, assumed to be an antecedent of tonicity, and high frequency cortical EEG patterns, indicative of higher cognitive activity (Liberson, 1967).

In the light of this concept, the classical psychoanalytical interpretation of the transition from primary to secondary processes (which represents the basis of the psychoanalytical theory of cognitive development) can be reevaluated. According to Rappaport's (1951) formulation:

> Ideation is the process by which a need causes the memory image of the need satisfying object to appear in consciousness. This hallucinatory experience and the accompanying affect discharge do not bring lasting gratification. Therefore the expenditure of cathexis in affect discharge and in making the memory-image hallucination vivid has to be prevented, that is, discharge must be delayed. Small amounts of the energy saved by this delay will be used by the thought process for finding the need-satisfying object in reality. [p. 324]

On the basis of sensoritonic theory the following model, explaining the genesis of secondary processes can be proposed. When a motor response leading originally to need satisfaction by direct contact with the need-satisfying object fails to provide satisfaction (because of absence or seclusion of the object) frustration results. This frustration may lead to two kinds of reactions:

1. The motor response is inhibited, involving cessation of innervation of the motor system. The organism withdraws to a state of passivity and motor inactivity in regard to the need-satisfying object. This motor "withdrawal" facilitates "regressive movement images" or hallucinatory imaginations of the object. In short, it gives rise to the "primary process."
2. If the frustration causes inhibition of the overt motor response *without* withdrawing the innervation of the motor response system, i.e., produces a state of suspended organismic tension or "action readiness," the free energy will be vicariously channeled (according to sensoritonic theory) and facilitate the arousal of reality-adapted movement representations. Such representations lead to a reality-adapted response that finally bring the organism into contact with the need-satisfying object by delay and detour and give rise to the "secondary process."

The crucial variable, then, in generating secondary processes is the maintenance of sensoritonic equilibrium at a certain level of action readiness (in spite of the preceding frustration of the direct motor response), so that reality-adapted movement representations can be vicariously activated. The mere hallucinatory imagination of the object as a temporary substitute satisfaction, as happens in dream and fantasy, and the subsequent delegation of "small amounts" of mental energy to find the object in reality, because the hallucinatory image is not gratifying enough, is not a sufficient explanation of the origin of secondary processes.

The important contribution of sensoritonic theory to the psychoanalytical interpretation of cognitive development is the introduction of sensoritonic alertness as a critical factor including secondary process. This sensoritonic alertness could be induced by "mild frustration," which does not provoke despair and diffuse motor discharge but is nevertheless strong enough to prevent the organism from withdrawing passively to hallucinatory imagination of need satisfaction. More in line with neopsychoanalytical, behavioristic, and Piagetian approaches, sensoritonic alertness appears to develop independently of frustration. According to these theories, the generation of inner tension, alertness and response readiness is "self-rewarding" and therefore leads to autoreinforcement and implicitly induces optimal tonicity for cognitive activity on the level of "secondary processes." Consequently, the organism will search for stimuli that increase or maintain sensoritonic tension, "motivated" by drives variously described as "nonhomeostatic," "exploratory," or "stimulus hunger".

Sensoritonic theory appears to provide a better conceptual framework to explain the etiology of various types of learning disabilities than psychoanalysis. Because psychoanalysis focuses on the conflicts between primary and secondary processes as the main source of learning failures, it may be appropriate in cases suffering predominantly from neurotic, psychopathic, or borderline psychotic disturbances. The many remaining types of learning problems linked with minimal organic brain damage, metabolic imbalances, endogenous, exogenous, and sociocultural mental retardation, and the various combinations of emotional and neurophysiological dysfunctions seem to be much better explained by sensoritonic theory.

Besides elucidating the role of sensoritonic equilibrium in reality adapted cognitive activity in general, sensoritonic theory provides a suitable framework to define the developmental dimensions of this equilibrium. This in turn may provide helpful in establishing important milestones of cognitive development, especially its psychobiological aspects. One developmental dimension of sensoritonic equilibrium is the change in the relative impact of extraneous, introceptive, and object stimulation with increasing age. Younger children are relatively overwhelmed by extraneous stimulation which is only weakly counteracted by adequate introceptive compensatory responses. This is experimentally evident in the effect of body tilt (extraneous stimulation) on the perception of the vertical, which in children under the age of 12 is perceived as tilted in the direction of body tilt (Wapner & Werner, 1957, p. 69).

This distorted perception of the position of the object stimulus seems to be the result of overdependency on "extraneous" stimulation, a sign of relative weakness in reality control resulting from immaturity. Indeed, in moments of stress, such weakness increases the tendency to fall in the direction of the tilt. This demonstrates that the child's perception of the vertical under the impact of body tilt is nonadaptive. Among brain-damaged patients whose sensoritonic equilibrium has been impaired a definite tendency to fall in the direction of extraneous stimulation can also be observed. In this context, the syndrome of "sensorimotor induction" observed in subjects with cerebral pathology should be mentioned (Halpern, 1949, 1956, 1963).

At the age of 12 a definitive shift in the ability to resist extraneous stimulation occurs, probably as a result of improved and more differentiated introceptive activity. Children over the age of 12 placed in tilted positions perceive the vertical as tilted in a direction opposite that of the tilt. In case of a threat to static balance, this facilitates compensatory corrective motor responses to reestablish postural equilibrium. This developmental shift may be interpreted as a more effective sensoritonic communication between nervous channels processing extraneous and introceptive information.

Another dimension of sensoritonic maturation is the growing ability to *inhibit immediate discharge of affective tension* in the form of impulsive acting out. The result of such control is not only the prevention of precocious and often maladaptive responses, but chiefly the sensoritonic redirection of mental and physiological energy into "vicarious" channels of "representative, virtual" motor activity that facilitate more differentiated, mediated, long-range cognitive functioning.

A third dimension of sensoritonic development would be the increase in sensoritonic tension generated either by physiological maturation or by greater efficiency of the neural feedback mechanisms which induce optimal levels of tonicity and alertness. Finally, it may be assumed that with progressing age a larger number of vicarious channels of extraceptive, intraceptive, and motor activity develop and differentiate, leading to a larger variety of sensoritonic states of equilibrium. These implicitly offer both a greater flexibility of sensorimotor adaptation and a broader basis for higher mental activity.

In this context, the developmental changes in transmodal transfer and intermodal integration should be mentioned. They seem to be intimately related to cognitive functions, especially to symbol formation and in a more specific sense, to reading ability (Birch & Belmont, 1965, Birch & Lefford, 1967; Vande Voort *et al.*, 1972). Although this subject has not been investigated in connection with sensoritonic theory, findings in this area seem to support the assumption that the increase of vicarious channeling of tonic tensions is a basic factor in the development of higher cognitive skills.

4

Biosemiotic Interpretations of Perceptual-Motor Processes and Their Involvement in Higher Cognitive Functions

Biosemiotic theory is based on a phenomenological analysis of human behavior and attempts to integrate experimental findings of neurophysiology, neuropsychiatry, experimental and clinical psychology, and comparative anatomy (Rothschild, 1958, 1961, 1962, 1963). According to the biosemiotic concept of the organism, the various centers, formations, areas, hemispheres, and tracts of the brain and nervous system are typically structured, shaped, positioned, and interlinked in such a way as to *symbolize* the purpose they serve. Actually, the interaction of these elements is interpreted as a "syntactic process" based on rules similar to those found in other communication systems, especially language. Accordingly, there is a similarity between the way motor sequences, visual images, and acoustic patterns are transformed (under the constraint of grammatical rules) into meaningful utterances and the way nervous circuits of varying complexity and scope (subordinated to the overall laws of purposeful adaptation to the stress of the environment) become "meaningful" in that they reflect the level, objective, and direction of organismic responses. Hence the term "biosemantics" or "biosemiotics" which designates an approach that attributes to biological and physiological processes the openness to obey rules of organismic syntax and grammar that are much like those explored by modern psycholinguistics.

The biosemiotic concept that the nervous system reflects the organism's adaptation to the environment as a dynamic expression of symmetry and possesses "ecologically relevant knowledge" of its surroundings is considerably supported by recent psychobiological and psychophysical models of cognition, such as those presented by Hockberg (1974), Shaw, McIntyre, and Mace (1974), and Shaw and McIntyre (1974). As for the semantic principles used by bio-semantic theory to interpret the interaction of nervous functions, the role of *context in modern semantics* and linguistic comprehension as elucidated by Bransford (1972), Bransford and McCarrell (1974), Franks and Bransford (1974) and Franks (1974) seem to justify the importance ascribed by biosemantic theory to the flexibility of roles and tasks of nervous centers and circuits according to the changing *context of neurological subsystems* involved in the varying patterns of adaptation to the "ecological" environment.

The higher on the phyletic scale, the more apparent the freedom in the organism's behavioral inventory. This freedom chiefly takes the form of its ability to organize nervous circuits into response hierarchies that are increasingly adaptive to more problematic situations and complex environmental pressures of low predictability. This freedom, however, is based on the evolution of the nervous system, anatomically separated from the rest of the body and thus having an "inner distance" from the other systems characterized by immediate response patterns to proximal stimulation only (Rothschild, 1963, p. 11). By virtue of this differentiation of the nervous system, "awareness," "experience," and "higher psychic processes" emerge.

In order to ensure the control of the vertebrate central nervous system (CNS) over the body, which has become "isolated" from the latter and thus functions "at some distance from the brain," a second, "peripheral" nervous system, supported by highly flexible hormonal communication channels, had to be developed to serve as a mediator or "interpreter." It either "translates" bodily needs and tensions into "pressures" and "moods" to be "understood" by the cerebral centers or receives messages from the sensory input system and renders them "meaningful" to the body by producing typical hormonal changes.

It is here assumed that a relationship exists between the "symbolic" arrangement and organization of the central and peripheral nervous systems and the emergence of inner psychic processes. These include the awareness of differences between external and internal events, the perception of time and space, the discrimination of past, present, and future, of subject and object, ego and nonego, etc. All these processes are actually antecedents and determinants of consciousness. Although the symbolic function of the CNS cannot be objectively observed and investigated, it can be used as a model and working hypothesis— testable as to its indirect consequences.

The biosemiotic method thus creates a bridge between phenomenogical approaches and introspective psychology (the latter providing the basis for clinical exploration and psychotherapy), and neurophysiology, biology, neuroanatomy, and communication theory, "moulding phenomenology and experimental sciences into a new union" (Rothschild, 1963, p. 34).

Biosemiotically, the general functions of the central nervous system can be interpreted as two-dimensional. These two dimensions are defined by Rothschild as "horizontal" and "vertical." Horizontally, the CNS is a mediator between the organism and its external environment. Vertically, it integrates somatic—visceral, sensorimotor, cognitive, and higher mental functions *within* the organism.

The biosemiotic approach will now be clarified by some examples of biosemiotic analysis of basic neuroanatomic structures and their "symbolic" relation to neurovegetative, preceptual, motor, and mental phenomena. Typical analogies and differences in neurological structure and behavior can be found by comparing various species at differing phyletic levels. For example, the spatial arrangements of afferent and efferent spinal nerves can be compared with respect to their function. It will be noted that the efferent nerves, which control movements, leave the spinal column on the ventral side—the direction not only of walk but also of all effective motor impulses. However the nervus accessorius, innervating the trapezius as well as the sternokleidomasteideus muscles—which raise and turn the head and thus may induce a reorientation of the body backwards—leave the spinal cord dorsally. This dorsal directedness of the nervus accessorious is more pronounced in vertebrates with long necks (such as lizards and birds) whose behavior involves frequent and flexible head turning. Nerves activating the muscles of the mouth and face, which have *inward* movement tendencies, form typical arcs between the CNS and their point of innervation. Such anatomic facts support the assumption that a relationship exists between the form and direction of the efferent nerve fibers and the pattern and tendency of the movement they induce. This could be viewed as a "symbolic" arrangement of the nervous channels, enabling the organism to "interpret" his motor impulses and to become aware of the directionality of his movements (Rothschild, 1958, pp. 31—33).

Another structural feature of the central nervous system to which biosemiotic theory ascribes great importance is the crossing over of nervous channels. "The cerebrum, the tectum of the mesencephalon and and nucleus ruber function in a cross-wise manner, whereas the cerebellum and the centers below the reticular formation, as well as tegmenti of the mesencephalon function homolaterally [Rothschild, 1958, p. 34]." Rothschild considers this structural division between homolaterally and crosslaterally functionning brain centers is the anatomical basis of the psychological process of subject—object differentiation.

An external object initially arouses the meso-diencephalic activation system, which transmits in a caudal direction through *homolateral* channels, leading to the innervation of the postural mechanisms. Thus the organism becomes motorically and tonically ready to "confront" the stimulus. In contrast, the same meso-diencephalic arousal is processed in cortical direction through the optical tracts to the visual cortex, this time innervating *crossed* channels. The difference between these two patterns of neurological information processing is supposed to enable the organism to differentiate between "subject" and "object." The homolateral innervation of the lower parts of the body produces the nucleus of "self-awareness," but the cephalically crosslaterally transmitted input evokes the primary image of an object, perceived as *extraneous* to the self and thus belonging to the outer world.

This dual aspect of the process of perceiving and knowing postulated by biosemiotic theory has recently become a central theme in cognitive psychology. Examples are the dichotomy between "peripheral" and "central" perceptual processes. Turvey (1973, 1974) has shown that is possible to differentiate between these two types of information processing by experiments in visual and auditory masking. When the masking is of central origin, the stimulus arriving later is more likely to be identified, i.e., masking of central origin is primarily backward.* Another theme is Gibson's theory of ecological optics which ascribes to the perceptual system the power to register—by means of "optical arrays"—invariant structures of stimulation "affording"† the observer direct knowledge of his environment (Gibson, 1966; Hochberg, 1974; Shaw, McIntyre, & Mace, 1974). "Constructive theory," in contrast, emphasizes the role of imaginative construction produced by complex internal brain functions and involving unconscious process that provoke dreams, hallucinations, and images (Gregory, 1972).†† Turvey (1974), however, indicates

> that in addition to detecting invariants, perceptual systems can be generative devices which construct perceptual experiences of certain kinds . . . [and] there is certainly an intimate and theoretically provocative relation between the workings of a perceptual system or a detector of invariances and the workings of a perceptual system as a generative device [p. 168].

Still another dual aspect of cognitive function is the difference between symbol manipulation systems and tacit, perceptually generated knowledge (Franks, 1974).

It is intriguing to speculate how far these cognitive and perceptual processes, which—by means of "optical arrays"—provide "direct ecological information" to the observer through "peripheral" sensory contact, are linked with *crossed*

---

*For a basic discussion of these investigations, see Kahneman (1968).

†The concept of *affordance* was introduced by Gibson (1966). Shaw *et al.* (1974) gives the following definition: "The affordances of events are those invariant properties which imply directly the meaningful dimensions of interaction an organism might have with his world."

††Constructive approaches are also needed to explore the "generative capacity" of perceptual systems and the processes of preconscious identification of objects without conscious awareness of their stimulus properties.

channels of the neural network. By contrast, how do the "generative," constructive, and symbolizing components of perceiving and knowing eventually relate to
the "subject" pole of the nervous system? According to biosemiotic theory,
these involve both the postural, "homologically innervated" apparatus and
cerebellar and mezencephalic functions.

An important part of biosemiotic theory is dedicated to the role of the so
called "virtual movements" in the differentiation of subject–object awareness, in
the establishment of reality control, and in the development of higher mental
functions. Virtual movements, which may also be labeled "movement representations" (Kohen-Raz, 1965) are planned or envisaged coordinated motor responses that the organism is actually capable of performing but prefers not to
under certain conditions. The muscles supposed to act are actually innervated
(Jacobson, 1932), but manifest motion is inhibited, and instead, a "representation," or "imagination" of the movement is evoked.

Palagyi (1925), who was the first to investigate the phenomenon of "virtual
movements," considers them to be basic components of space perception and
the anticipation of body and object displacements, as well as frames of reference
to estimate the duration, quality, and intensity of imminent motor responses in
general. These processes implicitly lead to the concept of an external universe of
objects opposed to a world of inner experiences. Rothschild, who fully accepts
Palagyi's theory, emphasizes in addition the role of static balance and postural
adjustment as core control mechanisms, without which overt motion could not
be efficiently restrained and, consequently, "virtual movements" could not be
generated. In this context, the cerebellum is considered to be the central
integrator and mediator between experiencing virtual motion and overt motor
performance (Rothschild, 1963). In this way, reality control is maintained.
Otherwise the organism would confound imagined and real movements and be
unable to utilize virtual movement to prepare for efficient motor action—as
actually happens in states of dizziness. "This differentiation achieved by means
of cerebellar function between the actual body movements activated by physical
drives on the one hand, and virtual movements transcending the body and linked
with spatial reality on the other, lead to a polarisation of the inner experience,
which generates the contrast between subject and object [Rothschild, 1958, p.
40]."

The cerebellum, by virtue of its role in generating "virtual movements" and
reintegrating them within the postural system, seems to be central to the
establishment of consciousness and reality control, as well as to the development
of cognitive functions, insofar as they are based on subject–object awareness
(i.e., freedom from egocentrism), alertness and attention, and orientation in
space and time.

The development of time and space awareness as well as the conceptualization
of past and future has been given special attention by biosemiotic theory.

According to Rothschild, the awareness of psychological *time* (not to be confused with physical time) is considered to be a *primary* psychological event. He assumes the typical rhythmic patterns of basic life functions provide the background of time awareness. For instance, the heart beat, respiration, and the sleep–wake cycle create a disturbance of homeostasis. In order to survive, the organism must "remember" either instinctual or learned responses that lead to the reinstatement of equilibrium. Upon recurrence of the disturbance, the organism will perform the tension-relieving response somewhat earlier, in anticipation. This process of remembering the response is the basis of experiencing the past and its anticipation is the basis of envisaging the future. The integration of these three very closely occurring events—disturbance of the vital background rhythm, evoked memory, and anticipation of relief—supported by the awareness of postural steadiness, generates the nucleus of the inner experience of continuity, which, in humans, is the basis of "ego function." It is this awareness of continuously experiencing events and their integration throughout *time* which guarantees the experience of ego integrity, areas within *space,* ego and self can be perceived as separate entities. Only after obtaining a core experience of psychological time is the concept of space able to be perceived. The medium that transforms the basic awareness of time into awareness of space is the virtual movement, already described. The notion of physical time, which is the basis of conventional measurement of time in science and everyday life, is the result of a secondary elaboration, in that regular displacements of objects perceived as moving evenly in space are subdivided into measurable segments.

According to Rothschild's theory how are these processes reflected "biosemiotically" in the structure of the CNS? The *diencephalon,* which includes the hypothalamus, known to be the center of primary drives (hunger, thirst, sex, reproduction), as well as general homeostasis, represents the organismic *past,* in that hereditary patterns as well as ontogenetic traces of past states of tensions and the experience of their subsequent reduction are stored there. However, these "drive reduction traces" and "response dispositions" have only nuclear dimensions of pure psychological time and must be linked to the spatial and temporal reality of the outside world by means of cortical intervention. In hypnotic states, in dreams, and in movements of imminent danger of death when diencephalic processes seem to overthrow cortical control, rescued subjects report experiences of flashbacks of whole life spans during a few seconds, i.e., within "diencephalically processed" time.

The lateral, occipital, central, and parietal lobes are believed to play a major role in the organization of space and structure of the past—this is assumed because of their linkage with the outside world via the visual and auditory distance perceptors and their respective receptive and associative areas. The visual sense seems to contribute essentially to the organization of space, and the auditive processes appear to be important in discrimination of time sequences. In addition to the aforementioned cerebral lobes, the tectum of the mesencephalon is believed to be an important monitor of perceptual processes linking external information with organismic "interpretations," being forwarded by impulses from the hypothalamus.

On the other hand, the structure of time, especially in the sense of predicting and programming the immediate or remote future—whether in the form of simple but skilled motor performances, execution of more elaborate sequential tasks, or complex mental problems—is assumed to be the central function of the *frontal* lobes (Pribram, 1969; Luria, 1973). Rothschild sees in the frontal position of the telencephalon (the center for anticipatory action) and the rear location of the diencephalon, mesencephalon, and most association areas (storing past experiences) another "symbolic" arrangement of the CNS organization.

Between the highly structured conceptualization of time and its cognitive derivations—apparently processed by the telencephalon and the frontal lobes, and between the diffuse, instinctual timing of experiences generated by the hypothalamic centers Rothschild ascribes an interesting mediatory role to the olfactory sense—unduly neglected by traditional as well as by current psychological research. Being on the one hand intensly aroused by external stimulation, but on the other hand, unconnected to the higher cerebral centers that provide exact information about the spatial and temporal position of the external stimulus, olfactory activity is unable to guide directly consumatory behavior. However, through direct connections with the thalamus and by means of specific arousal mechanisms, drive tension generated by olfaction is not directly discharged but evokes "searching behavior," well-known in animals under the name of "appetence" (Craig, 1918). It is this "provocation" of search, trial and error, which seems to be an important precursor of oriented, planned, and purposive behavior in animals as well as in humans. It seems that the nucleus amygdalae, which is a part of the telencephalon, is involved in the generation of "expectancy" and "alertness" concomitant with explorative behavior. (These nuclei are highly developed in whales and bats, which excel in their ability to move fast and safely through space under a radar guidance of a suprasonic feedback system.)

As to higher cognitive functions, namely the versatile use of human language as a tool of scientific thought, the ability of insight and moral judgment, and the like, Rothschild considers the development of a dominant and a nondominant hemisphere as the decisive phylogenetic step predisposing the human CNS to such achievements. In the same manner as psychological processes of inner awareness, time and space perception, sensorimotor skill, and so on have become differentiated from cellular and vegatative functions by virtue of the development of the CNS, human higher mental functions have assumedly emerged through the following additional ways of differentiation of the latter: (*a*) more numerous bilateral nerve crossings; (*b*) enlargement of the cortical area; (*c*) increased interconnections between the thalamic and cortical centers; (d) intensification of intramodal linkages; (e) prominent involvement of the frontal lobes; (f) establishment of hemispheric dominance.

These excerpts from biosemiotic theory, which treats many other features of the nervous system (such as the direction of brain folds and layers, the position of the cerebellum, the medulla, and the mesencephalon) are sufficient to demonstrate its potential contribution to a better understanding of psychobiological problems of development in general and of cognitive development in particular.

Because of their emphasis on comparing *developmental levels* of the CNS in various species and its focus on the symbolic meaning of *interaction* processes between brain centers in relation to *overall* behavior rather than fragmentary physiological correlates of behavioral segments, the principles of biosemiotic theory seem to be widely applicable to the investigation of linkages between neurophysiological growth and cognitive development.

According to biosemiotic theory, motor activity is "internalized" through the establishment of "virtual movements," which in turn are antecedents and constituents of reality-adapted perception, sensory motor activity, and even higher cognitive processes. This assumption has been investigated by several authors.

Senden's (1960) well-known experiments with congenitally blind adults whose retinal images had to be structured by motor and haptic experience before their sight became adequate support the theory that realistic perception is based on the integration of visual input and "virtual movements." In this context, a case history cited by Gregory (1966, p. 194) of a cataract patient whose vision was restored at an advanced age and who had been deprived of any previous visual experience is highly instructive. The case demonstrates again that visual space orientation gained under such circumstances is heavily dependent on haptic cues, including those experienced before the operation. Moreover, such late induction of motor cues into the visual field seemed to be stressful and tiresome, to such an extent that the patient preferred to explore objects in darkness.

Köhler's (1964) studies on spatial reorientation of the retinal image by wearing inverting or distorting prisms point in a similar direction. Recent experiments on the effects of prismatic distortion have been carried out by Wallace (1974). His results support the "motor theory of perception" in that the execution of directed movements (preexposure pointing), the observation of arm movements (reafference during exposure), and presumably involvement of oculomotor feedback (location of the object at the periphery rather than the center of the visual field) have also been shown to facilitate visual reorientation under circumstances of artificially distorted space perception.

The involvement of motor experience in the establishment of "reality adaptation" in animals has been demonstrated by Held (1965), who compared the behavior of kittens harnessed in a gondola and passively moved around by other kittens which drove the carousel on which the gondola was mounted. As predicted the animals deprived of motor experience showed definitive postexperimental inferiority in sensorimotor skill. Similar results were obtained with humans, wearing distorting lenses; those who were moved around in wheel chairs adapted much more slowly to the distorted visual field than those who walked and pushed them (Held, 1965). From a somewhat different angle, the same author has recently investigated the effects of mobile cues on space perception (Held et al. 1975).

Among the pioneer investigators of the problem was Uexküll (1926) who noted:

> The "action habit" (Handlungsregel) serves as frame of reference to the sensory cues and becomes integrated with them. Only by virtue of this process are real objects perceived in the world of sensations (Merkwelt) possessing rules of function (Funktionsregel): . . . This leads to the methodological necessity of investigating the motor reaction in its interplay with perceptions. [p. 133] *"

Piaget's description of sensorimotor intelligence lends itself to interpretation by "virtual movement theory"; i.e., primary and secondary circular reactions are obvious manifestations of intensive self-stimulative motor exercises in handling and manipulating objects while experiencing visual, auditory, and proprioceptive feedback. The integration of these motor activities and multisensory impressions fosters the ability to conceive object displacements realistically and to understand the permanence of objects out of reach and sight.

Two examples of Piaget's observations will be cited.

> When the 9–10-month-old baby is placed between two pillows and he has succeeded in finding an object hidden and placed under the right one, the object can be taken from his hands and placed under the left pillow before his very eyes, but he will look for it under the right pillow where he has already found it once before, as if the permanence of the object were connected with the success of the former action, and not with a system of external displacements in space. [1951, p. 164]

At an intermediate stage, before succeeding in this task at approximately 11 months, Piaget (1954, p. 53) observed that the child found the toy under the second pillow if he was stretching out his hands towards the object (without touching it, however).

In another observation, Piaget described a child trying to open a match box. During his trial, the child opens and closes his mouth, according to Piaget's

---

*These experiments and considerations indicate that movement alone, in the absence of the opportunity for recognition of error, does not suffice to produce adaptation; it must be self-produced movement. That is, according to Held, the correlation entailed in the sensory feedback accompanying movement—reafference—plays a vital role in perceptual adaptation.

interpretation demonstrating a midway stage between imitation and internalization of movements (Piaget, 1949, p. 242).*

The role of virtual movements in the structurization of skilled or overlearned motor performance has been aptly described by Bartlett (1958).

> Skilled performance must all the time submit to receptor control and be initiated and directed by the signals which the performer must pick up from his environment, in combination with other signals of his own body, which tell him something about his own movements as he makes them. It is these hoverings and halts which are the most important regulators of the "timing" which characterizes smooth and efficient skilled performances [p. 17].

However, evidence contradicting the "virtual movement theory" has been corroborated by recent investigations based on different lines of approach. Fantz (1961) and McKenzie and Day (1971) have demonstrated very early visual pattern discrimination that probably could not have been acquired by experience of overt or "virtual" motion in two month old infants. The saccadic localization of visual targets with differential efficacy along horizontal, vertical, and diagonal axes in 1-month-old babies demonstrated by Aslin and Salapatek (1975) can also hardly be attributed to acquired internalization of motor experience.

Other observations apparently at variance with theories linking sensorimotor intelligence to primary internalization of limb movements are reports on physical and cognitive growth of thalidomide children born with deformed or missing extremities and unable to explore their environment by hand–eye coordination. Nevertheless, they have shown normal mental development (Pringle, 1970). In a recent study, Bruner (1972) observed differential patterns of anticipatory grasp and reaching with objects of varying sizes, in infants at the prereaching stage who could not have shaped their response by haptic experience.

Even in light of these findings, the virtual movement theory may still be defended by the assumption that babies unable or not mature enough to control and activate their arms and hands, vicariously use their neck muscles and oculomotor responses to build up a control and feedback system of "virtual movements."

Another aspect of biosemiotic theory recently investigated empirically, is the role of static balance ability in cognitive growth. It will be recalled that according to the biosemiotic model the control of body posture is not only a coordinated effort to counteract the pull of gravity but also a mechanism of anchorage that restrains motor impulses from being discharged in actual motion

---

*Obviously, Piaget's interpretation may be erroneous, as reflexes and innate response inventories play an important role in movements of the oral apparatus. The example is presented because it is several times re-cited by Piaget himself as an example of earliest action internalisation.

and transforms them into "virtual movements." On the basis of these assumptions, a relationship between postural control and cognitive function was postulated. The hypothesis was supported, in that correlations between static balance ability (as measured by a specially designed method of electronic ataxiametry) and cognitive school readiness was found (Kohen-Raz, 1970). Details of the study and method of investigation are described on page 60.

Exercises designed to train static and dynamic balance, such as standing on tiptoe, balancing on bars, or walking along narrow rails are found in remedial physical training programs (Cratty, 1969; Delacato, 1966; Kephart, 1965). The direct effect of balance training on cognitive skills, however, is questionable (Kohen-Raz, 1972; Cratty, 1970).

Also, the relationship between muscle tonicity (which, according to biosemiotic theory is linked with the experience of self-assertion in confrontation with the outside world) and mental development, especially in infants, deserves attention. Both spastic paralysis and muscular flacidity are frequently found in babies suspected of being mentally retarded. It is difficult to establish to what extent muscle tonicity and infantile mental development are interrelated and to what extent dysfunctions of the nervous system impair both tonicity and cognition. The possible involvement of "physiological tonicity" in facilitating cognitive processes has been discussed by Liberson (1967), in the context of exploring the impact of diencephalic arousal on cortical EEG patterns.

As for the role of the frontal lobes in time perception and planning future action postulated by biosemiotic theory, Pribram (1969) demonstrated a specific difficulty in frontally ablated monkeys to perform a variety of sequential tasks. He comments that "the anterior frontal cortex supplies a mechanisms that decodes the flow of events by inserting 'pauses' at the appropriate time, thus providing a grammar, as it were, for the psychological process and behavior [p. 219]." He compares the role of the anterior frontal cortex to the function of "executive routines" in computer programs that determine the priority and sequence of events to be processed. (With such routines, "time sharing," i.e., the use of a single computer by many users, has become possible.) These findings throw light on the importance of frontal lobe functions in the development of higher cognitive skills which are present in many respects in the analysis and discrimination of temporal sequences.

These examples of recent research demonstrate that biosemiotic theory may serve as a convenient theoretical framework for exploring psychobiological aspects of cognitive growth in various areas and at various developmental phases. It can also be seen that the conceptual framework of biosemiotic theory facilitates interdisciplinary approaches and cooperation in this area and seems to provide a convenient basis for empirical research and analysis in the fields of developmental psychology and neurology, behavioral genetics, and special education.

5

Psychobiological Aspects of
Cognitive Development in Infancy

This discussion of psychobiological aspects of cognitive growth in infancy does not focus on general relationships between the intensive maturation of the central nervous system during the first year of life and its easily observed behavioral correlates (Milner, 1967). Nor is it a survey of the rationale and techniques of neurological diagnosis in infancy—which provides a wealth of information about linkages between typical impairments of neurological functions and measurable psychomotor and perceptual deficits (Paine & Oppé, 1966; Prechtl & Touwen, 1970; Rutter, Graham, & Yule, 1970). The chapter deals, rather, with a restricted number of problems; it discusses some critical phases of cognitive growth in infancy and their estimated physiological correlates. It includes some observations on the nature–nurture interaction in processes of infantile perception and cognition based on some recent experimental approaches. It concludes with a discussion of the problems of EEG measurements as they relate to cognitive growth in infancy and to the eventual role of tonicity and metabolic processes in early mental development.

CRITICAL PHASES IN THE DEVELOPMENT OF
SENSORIMOTOR INTELLIGENCE

Among the first phases of cognitive development seem to be the infant's intentional visual pursuit of objects moving across his visual field and his scanning of contours and geometrical figures, already manifest during the first hours of life (Kessen & Herschenson, 1963; Kessen, Salapatek, & Haith, 1972; Salapatek & Kessen, 1966, 1973; Salapatek, 1968). There is also evidence on early, reliable, directionally appropriate first search toward peripherally perceived objects at one month of age (Aslin & Salapatek, 1975).

These early visual following and scanning responses are not only signs of intact vision but also manifestations of complex feedback mechanisms regulating the cerebral registration of the visual stimulus and the corresponding eye movements. They ensure that the stimulus remains in the focal area of the retina and probably also inform the organism about the "extraneous" character of the stimulus (Pritchard, 1961). The neurophysiological processes linked with this primary sensorimotor performance are not yet known, but investigations in this area are presently in progress (Bruner, personal communication).

In this context, another basic problem of early cognitive development is encountered, namely, the nature of primary form perception. Prevalent environmentalistic theories and approaches strongly opposed the Gestalt theory of "isomorphism" between patterns of neural circuits and "innate perception of Gestalten." Recent experiments, although not providing direct evidence on "innate figures" perceived below 1 and 2 months of age, demonstrate very early visual pattern discrimination of size, number, orientation, and circularity (Fantz, 1961; McKenzie & Day, 1971).

These results support the assumption that some rudimentary form of pattern perception is either innate or learned very early by differential interaction between retinal stimulation and proprioceptive feedback from eye muscle movements involved in primary visual tracking and pursuit.

It is possible that these primary pattern discriminations are hereditary, in that they are similar to the visual "releasing schemata" in animals and to the motor schemata like sucking, "stepping," and "swimming" also manifest in the human newborn. It then may be asked whether experience during infancy leads to a gradual elaboration of these primary perceptions or they are deleted or superimposed by acquired perceptual habits that may resemble the way early swimming and stepping movements in human infants are suppressed and replaced by voluntary, coordinated motor skills.

Another decisive phase of infantile cognitive development is the stage of the "secondary circular reactions," as they are called in Piaget's terminology. This stage is characterized by the child's striving to reproduce "an interesting spectacle" by means of his own body activity, for example, shaking a toy suspended over the crib by kicking (Piaget, 1953). It will be noted that such repeatedly "self-produced stimulation" does not lead to a consumatory act (such as intake of food) but seems to be "intrinsically" self-rewarding. Bruner (1973) systematically evoked "secondary circular reactions" by using the infant's sucking response to focus or unfocus pictures projected on a screen by means of an electronic device. Although Bruner's experiments demonstrated that infants as young as 9-13 weeks (i.e., at "prereaching" stage) are able to discriminate between blurred and clear pictures (which supports the assumption that primary form discrimination is independent of haptic experience), no systematic research has yet been undertaken to explain the possible neurophysiological correlates of these cognitive achievements. Obviously, a transmodal integration of visual and proprioceptive input systems must be accomplished in order to produce "secondary circular reactions." The absence or weakness of secondary circular reactions easily observed in infants with CNS impairments may help to discover the neurological sources of the transmodal synergies required to perform at this cognitive level.

Reaching, based on differentiated hand–eye coordination, represents the next important step in the development of sensorimotor intelligence. This developmental phase has recently been investigated in great detail by Flament (1963), White, Castle, and Held (1964), and Bruner (1972). White, Castle, and Held describe a sequence of 10 phases in the development of intentional reaching, starting with "peripheral pursuit," proceeding through intermediate steps such as "central pursuit, hand regard, alternating glances, bilateral arm activity, hand fumbling at object," and terminating with "top level reach." Certain aspects of White, Castle, and Held's analysis of the reaching response have been verified from a different angle and by a different method. Applying Guttman's scalogram analysis to normative infant test data, antecedents to unilateral reaching described by these authors, such as "alternating glances" turned out to form scalable sequences with the fully developed reaching responses (Kohen-Raz, 1967).

Bruner's study focused on the problem of anticipatory coordination of arm and hand movements, *preceding* the actual act of reaching. He used babies still at the "prereaching" stage who consequently could not have corrected or differentiated their anticipatory responses by visual and tactile feedback while grasping the object. As Bruner's results demonstrate, infants at the age of 4 months perform differently when balls of varying sizes are presented to them. This may indicate that basic patterns of visually coordinated reaching responses are to a certain extent "preformed" and not exclusively the result of learning by trial and error.

Again, no straightforward evidence about the physiological correlates of these data is yet available. The minute analysis of the antecedent and concomitant sensorimotor elements involved in the act of reaching as described by White, Castle, and Held and Bruner do suggest, however, that (in part at least) genetically "preprogramed" schemata are involved, which by virtue of maturation and learning are converted into sequences of coordinated and effective response patterns.

While these studies on the development of reaching in the human infant carried out by White, Castle, and Held (1964) have provided a delineation of "levels" and minute "stages" in the development of reaching behavior, another study by White and Held (1966) demonstrated the flexibility of this development, in that the level of "top reaching" (the last stage of the developmental sequence of reaching) can be attained earlier when the infant is stimulated by appropriate exercise and exposure to stimulating objects. There is also evidence on the adverse effects of institutionalization on reaching behavior (Kohen-Raz, 1966). These findings are supported by results of deprivation experiments on monkeys, artificially restricted in the development of visually guided reaching and grasping (Held & Bauer, 1967).

It also seems that the mastery of erect posture plays a certain role in the development of this basic sensorimotor skill. This is suggested by clinical observations of delayed reaching behavior in infants with congenital hip dislocation whose sitting and standing were temporarily impeded by restricting the movement of their lower extremities with splints. After removal of the splints, hand—eye coordination and reaching seemed to develop rapidly and to catch up with normative performance level (Kohen-Raz & Russel, in preparation).

In this context Wilson's recently presented data should be mentioned, which suggest a linkage between the mechanisms of balance plus the impetus to attain upright posture and mobility assessed at infancy, with the overall cognitive mechanisms tested by the Binet intelligence test at the age of 3 years. The relationship seems to be influenced not only by accumulated experience, but also by inherent biological factors as well (Wilson, 1976).

The next presumably "critical" phase in the infant's cognitive development is characterized by the appearance of voluntary bilateral coordination of both hands at the age of 6—8 months. It is seen in such responses as simultaneously grasping two objects, one in each hand, and "midline skills" such as clapping hands. Phases of bimanual activity were systematically observed by Gesell, who describes them as parts of a rhythmic sequence of alternating stages of unilaterality and bilaterality, appearing during the first year of life. (He reports bilaterality at 24 weeks, a shift to unilaterality at 28 weeks, a shift back to bilaterality at 32 weeks and at 36 weeks return to unilaterality [Gesell & Ames, 1947].)

Bimanual activity at the age of 6—8 months, however, seems to be of particular significance. It has been shown to be related to the child's overall mental and motor development. To demonstrate this relationship, exact measures of bimanual skill were taken, such as latency of bilateral grasp and frequence of bimanual interaction during brief time samples. Furthermore, in a measurement of the number of bimanual transfers of 1-inch cubes from hand to hand during a 3-minute interval, significant relationships with scores on a Guttman scale measuring the attainment of object permancy (in Piaget's sense) were obtained (Kohen-Raz, 1966).

It was also found that the item "transfers object from hand to hand" forms a scalable sequence with items such as "uncovers hidden toy," "unwraps cube," and others. Institutionalized infants, whose delay in mental and motor development is notorious, showed systematic and consistent retardation in bimanual coordination.* These data seem to suggest that bimanual coordination during the age period of 6–8 months is an easily measurable stage of motor and mental growth that represents a necessary precursor of the notion of object permanence. This level of mental skill, defined by Piaget as the fourth stage of sensorimotor intelligence, is also closely related to Piaget's "tertiary circular reactions," the latter consisting in the ability to differentiate between "means" and "objectives." The basic importance of this stage in early mental development is well appreciated by most investigators of child and infant psychology, irrespective of their approach or method. Because it is linked with a phase of maturation of coordinated bilateral manipulation, it may throw light on possible ways to investigate the neurophysiological aspects of this critical phase. This phase may be determined by the maturation and functional increase of neural interconnections between the cerebral hemispheres and by the emergence of hemisphere dominance. Both processes are considered by biosemiotic theory to represent decisive steps toward the typical "human" functioning of the central nervous system. (See page 37.)

In this context, investigations of patients after section of the cerebral commisures or children with agenesis of the corpus callosum may be relevant. They provide important information on the differentiation of the two hemispheres (Gazzaniga, Bogen, & Sperry, 1967; Loeser & Alvord, 1968; Sperry, 1964). Findings seem to indicate that innate or surgical disconnection of the hemispheres does not impair intelligence and language functions so long as the dominant hemisphere is engaged in the sensorimotor or mental task (which is not the case when the nondominant hemisphere is left on its own preventing sensory input to the dominant half of the brain). Still there might be a general decrease of what Grey Walter describes as the "double storage buffer function" of hemispheric interaction, which seems to be linked with selection and storage of information in the human cerebrum (Sperry & Gazzaniga, 1967, p. 117). In the context of the role of bimanual manipulation in cognitive development at the age of 6–8 months, it would be important to investigate these responses in infants with agenesis of the corpus callosum. Unfortunately, most of these cases seem to suffer from additional cerebral pathology which alone would account for their mental and motor retardation, while the relatively few with apparent normal mental development are unlikely to be diagnosed until they have passed their infancy (Loeser & Alvord, 1968).

A different aspect of attaining the notion of object permanence has been

*It has recently been demonstrated that culturally disadvantaged infants also show a conspicuous developmental lag in this ability (Ela, 1973).

demonstrated by Woodward (1959, 1963), who investigated patterns of intellectual functioning in idiots at mental levels below 2 years. Her study showed that the notion of object permanence precedes the intentional use of language in meaningful utterances. None of the severely retarded subjects who lacked the notion of object permanence was able to use meaningful verbal expressions. This sequential pattern of the infant's cognitive development has been also demonstrated by Gouin-Décarie (1965) and postulated by Frankenstein (1966).

All three authors view this developmental sequence as a psychosocial process. It is assumed that the mother is not only a "primary love object" but also the major source of the basic experience of trust and stability, embodying the notion that an object from the external world continues to exist and eventually reappears in spite of being temporarily out of view or touch. This experience is the "emotional" basis for the cognitive process of conceiving object permanence. In addition, the knowledge that objects exist in spite of being beyond the range of vision, touch, or hearing seems to be the precondition for establishing the notions of referents to which speech is related. Obviously, speech is in turn stimulated by social contact with the mother or caretaker. We would thus observe the sequence "the near mother"* → object permanence → object permanence plus near mother → verbal communication.

It must be asked whether, indeed, this developmental sequence is primarily the result of mother–child interaction or equally (at least in part) determined by psychobiological growth.† It is possible that this sequence is the result of a progressive intermodal integration, starting with unilateral reaching based on the integration of tactual and visual input. Bilateral reaching appears to involve intensified interaction of the hemispheres and increased proprioceptive feedback. These in turn, facilitate the memory and imagination of trajectories ("virtual movements") of objects disappearing behind screens and obstacles, i.e., mental processes leading to the notion of object permanence. Finally, speech requires the integration of auditory signals with other information, transmitted through visual, tactile, and proprioceptive modalities of integration, presumably based on the maturation of the dominant hemisphere. This would result in meaningful verbalization, referring to "permanent objects" as referents. The fact that the infant's manipulative play is affected by controlled audiovisual reinforcement at ages 9–11 months supports this assumption (Leuba & Friedlander, 1968), but Rapaport (1969) has described a case of congenital sensory

---

*This concept was coined by Frankenstein (1966) and refers to the child's experience to trust that the temporarily absent mother will return.

†Scarr-Salapatek (1976) explains that "the development of social attachments is intertwined with increasing cognitive skills, such as object and person permanence [p. 167]." She considers this integrative process to be phylogenetically rooted, as it represents the basis for survival for the primate and human infant.

neuropathy where normal speech and verbal comprehension developed in the complete absence of tactile afference.

This case could be compared with that of Helen Keller. The two cases present a diametrically opposed and quasi-complementary constellation of deficits in functions considered vital to language development—vision, hearing, kinesthetic feedback, tactile experiences, movement imagination, and mental representation of permanent objects. Although the latter function is intact in both cases, Helen Keller was deprived of the first two but attained extraordinary competence in the remaining three. Rapaport's case was neither blind nor deaf but did not experience kinesthetic feedback and tactile input, presumably encountering difficulties in movement representations. Nevertheless, both were able to attain mastery in symbol formation and linguistic communication at a normal level.

In this context, observations on children with severe motor impairments who nevertheless developed normal symbolic functions should be mentioned (Kopp & Shaperman, 1973). Scarr-Salapatek (1976) attempts to explain the relative independence in the development of sensorimotor skills and symbol formation by phylogenetic differentiation. Sensorimotor intelligence, which seems to be universally mastered by all nondefective humans and primates during infancy, has evolved earlier in our primate past than symbolic behavior, which is acquired only between the ages of 2 and 14 years, whereas its higher forms (i.e., formal reasoning) are never attained by many human individuals.

This reappraisal of the first main phases of infant mental development from a psychobiological point of view must be considered tentative and speculative, given the present state of knowledge. It is to be hoped that methods will become available to test these assumptions and gain information on the more subtle relations between neurological growth and sensorimotor intelligence in normal and developmentally impaired infants.

EEG STUDIES IN INFANCY

Electroencephalogram studies of infants have focused either on describing general developmental patterns of electrical brain activity in normal subjects, (Dreyfus-Brisac, 1966) or on analyzing abnormal records, helping to detect cerebral nerve damage as early as possible (Pain & Oppé, 1966). No systematic research on linkages between EEG patterns and the attainment of well-defined levels or stages of normal infantile cognitive development are known to us, although several studies deal with relationships between EEG and intellectual and perceptual performance in normal older children and adults (Giannitrapani, 1969; Knott & Friedman, 1942; Vogel & Broverman, 1968). Pampiglione (1971) has demonstrated typical age progress in EEG records of infants characterized by abruptness and drastic alterations of patterns.

Whether these marked transitions between developmental stages of the EEG are related to the phases of sensorimotor intelligence is an intriguing question. Pampiglione (1971) also draws attention to ethnic differences in developmental EEG patterns during the first two years of life, a rather unexpected phenomenon. Although this requires statistical control of ethnic background variables in electroencephalic studies of infancy, it may offer fresh insight into the etiology of cognitive deficits in socioculturally deprived ethnic groups.

Bates (1951) registered EEG correlates of the beginning of voluntary responses. However, an EEG study of 20 thalidomide babies carried out by Pampiglione and Quibell (1966) showed that the lack of afference from fingers, hands, and arms (believed to be essential components in the development of sensorimotor skills), and even the absence of all four limbs did not seem to influence the developmental pattern of the EEG between the ages of 2 and 4. In the area of perceptual development, Karmel and Hoffman (1974) recently succeeded in showing linkages between the contour density of checkerboard-like stimulus figures visually explored by young infants and variations in the peak amplitude ($P2$) of simultaneously recorded evoked potentials.

Extension of research along these lines has revealed a preference for greater, contour density as age progresses. This preference (as quantitatively assessed by a special index) consistently predicts the maximum amplitude component of the visually evoked potential (VEP) in 2–14-month-old infants. In the context of these investigations "primary" and "nonprimary" neuronal systems were discovered to be involved in early attention to patterned visual stimuli. The "nonprimary" system, linked with cortical projection and association areas, was found not to be functional before 6 weeks of age. It was also postulated that this neuronal activity underlying visually evoked potentials is related to mechanisms of oculomotor control and feedback, thus ensuring the child's continuous attention to and effective inspection of visual patterns. (Karmel & Maisel, 1975).

These results represent a major stride in the area of research on infant VEP, which previously had been limited to investigations on effects of unpatterned stimuli (Ellingson, 1967). They also shed new light on the neurological bases of primary cognitive processes.

TONICITY AND METABOLISM

Another area of investigation pertinent to the explanation of psychobiological determinants of cognitive growth in infants is the relationship between cognitive growth and muscular tonicity. Aside from the fact that infants with hypotonicity show mental and motor retardation (an example is the typical hypotonicity in mongoloid babies), no systematic evidence on causal links between tonicity and mental activity in infants has yet been presented. One of the difficulties in determining the existence of such linkage is the fact that a central cerebral dysfunction may be the common cause of both abnormal tonicity and deficient mental ability, both of which seem to occur in most clinically deviant cases. As already mentioned (p. 41), the general effects of tonicity on cognitive functions were postulated by Liberson (1967) in the context of EEG investigations focusing on the relationship between subcortical arousal and electrical cortical activity. No infant studies on this subject, however, are known to us.

Finally, research dealing with metabolic functions in infancy should be taken into consideration as a possible source of information about psychobiological aspects of infant cognitive growth. There is well-supported evidence of the detrimental effects of metabolic disorders on cerebral functions, as in the case of phenylketonuria. We still lack insight as to eventual positive impacts of metabolic processes on intellectual development, although findings related to the "birth season effect" (see Chapter 7) provide some indirect evidence in this direction.

DISTINGUISHING ORGANIC AND CULTURAL RETARDATION

In concluding this chapter, an attempt will be made to describe some clinical signs that seem to differentiate sociocultural from neurologically determined types of retarded or delayed mental and motor development in infancy. It must be pointed out that these diagnostic criteria are based on clinical impressions of a small number of cases.* Therefore they must be merely considered tentative and suggestive, eventually providing clues for further systematic investigations on large samples.

"Pure sociocultural neglect" is manifest chiefly in a conspicuous delay of imitative activity which, as shown by scalogram analysis (Kohen-Raz, 1967), is a necessary antecedent of verbal understanding and receptive language. Consequently, vocalization and expressive language are also retarded. Such retardation, however, can be found in otherwise normal but overprotected, middle class children, as well as in various types of language disturbances. In itself it is not a reliable sign for the diagnosis of early cultural deprivation. Gross motor development (sitting, standing) in disadvantaged infants may show developmental lags of 2–4 months, but it can be suspected that any longer delay is caused by organic factors. Inferiority in unilateral and bilateral reaching, on the other hand, seem to be a sensitive indicator of sociocultural retardation at ages 4 to 7 months, as shown by a recent investigation (Ela, 1973). On the other hand, neither free manipulation of objects nor fine motor coordination as measured by prehension

*The material presented in this section is based on the total case referrals to the Jerusalem Child and Family Development Center over a period of 6 months in 1971.

of small cubes and pellets seems to be affected by cultural neglect. The latter function is typically impaired in infants with suspected "minimal brain damage" or more severe cerebral disturbances.

In connection with other early "soft" signs of neurological deficiencies, lack of symmetry in strength, poor scope and efficiency of motor performance, and weakness of bimanual coordination must first be mentioned. Free manipulation of objects is slow, often stereotypic. Imitation, vocalization, and general language development are delayed, but, in contrast to the delay apparent in the culturally disadvantaged, resistance to treatment and failure to respond to stimulation are much stronger. As already stated, retardation of more than four months in gross motor functions is indicative of organic mental deficiency.

Another difference between cultural and organic retardation that appears longitudinally during the first 15 months is a more or less constant discrepancy between actual and expected mental level, i.e., a relatively constant, albeit low, IQ in the culturally disadvantaged in contrast to the increasing developmental lag (i.e., decreasing IQ) in cases with organic dysfunction. The more severe the deterioration of the IQ, the more serious the suspected cerebral damage.

Using level of DQ alone as a discriminant variable, distributions of clinical types presented on Table 1 were obtained. These data are based on a comparison of the developmental quotients and pediatric diagnosis of 44 cases (the total current intake of the Jerusalem Child and Family Development Center during a period of 11 months). It will be observed that in most infants with severe developmental lag (DQ below 59), pediatric examination either clearly demonstrated impairment of the central nervous system or suggested that such impair-

Table 1

Relationship between Developmental Quotients on the Bayley Mental Scale and Pediatric Diagnosis[a]

Pediatric diagnosis	Developmental quotients[b]		
	87 and above (normal)	86–60 (slight to moderate retardation)	59 and below (severe retardation)
Various handicaps not related to CNS damage	12	4	0
Pure environmental deprivation	4	2	4
Environmental deprivation plus physical problems	9	2	1
Clear signs of CNS damage	2	3	5
Suspected CNS damage	0	2	3
Totals	*18*	*13*	*13*

[a]From Kohen-Raz, Russel, and Ornoy (1976).
[b]Chronological age of infants: 3–32 months.

ment is highly probable. The babies scoring low on the infant test without showing any signs of neurological deviations suffered from grave environmental neglect. Most children with handicaps not directly affecting the central nervous system, such as partial blindness, hearing deficits, gastrointestinal troubles, congenital heart diseases, or peripheral malformations performed normally on the Bayley Mental Scales. Finally, the incidence of normal development despite environmental deprivation should be noted.

In consideration of the findings, speculations, and general considerations presented in this chapter, it must be admitted that relative to the vast efforts dedicated to infant research in both neurophysiology and behavioral sciences only hints and educated guesses about linkages between physiological and mental development in infancy have been gleaned. Considerable access to possible avenues of approach has been gained, however, and the results of pilot efforts in the areas described in the preceding sections are promising.

6

Psychobiological Aspects
of School Readiness*

School readiness, operationally defined as the child's ability to learn the first grade curriculum, and his willingness to adjust to the social demands and pressures of a classroom setting, has at least three different aspects: (*a*) intellectual maturity, demonstrated by the child's gradual mastery of "concrete operational reasoning" which is gaining a definitive priority over more primitive, "magic" and "intuitive" forms of thought; (*b*) emotional emancipation from dependence on parental figures, leading to increasing openness to social interaction with social agents outside the family, namely, teachers and peers; (*c*) control of affects and impulses to the extent of being able to bear frustrations and tensions generated by relatively difficult and long-range tasks and endeavors.

It is generally agreed that the level of school readiness as a measurable criterion must be defined according to the age of compulsory school entrance and the official requirements of the first grade curriculum (Dey, 1958). It has also been recognized that, whatever the established level of school readiness, chronological age alone is not a satisfactory predictor (Ilg, Ames, & Apell, 1965).

For this reason, various tests or batteries of school readiness tests have been developed to screen children shortly before school entrance age in an attempt to predict their prospective scholastic success or failure (Hetzer & Tent, 1958; Ilg & Ames, 1965; Johansson, 1965; Rey, 1952). Contrary to what might be expected, physical and psychobiological aspects of school readiness have been relatively neglected by theoretical and applied research. In practice, even elementary

*Parts of this chapter have been presented in the context of the Sarah Stolz Lecture 1974, Guy's Hospital, London, and published in Guy's Hospital Reports, 1976.

physical and neurological examinations are rarely included in routine procedures of school readiness assessment. This chapter discusses this issue more closely.

First, it should be noted that in all countries that have introduced compulsory education, school entrance age has been fixed between ages five and seven (Ilg & Ames, 1965; Johansson, 1965). In societies that have no institutionalized educational system, children at ages 6 to 7 also tend to restrict their free play activities and begin to learn new tasks and roles that either prepare them for adult economic life or engage them directly in adult chores and duties (Mead, 1949). This nearly universal practice of starting to teach skills needed for later work and vocation to children at an age period broadly similar in many societies and cultures supports the assumption that the "school" or "work" readiness manifest in these age groups is essentially the result of maturation, a process in which neurological and biological factors are necessarily involved.

While no anthropological data on preliterate societies are available that would support this assumption, some attempts have been made to assess physical criteria of school readiness in Western countries. Zeller (1952) proposed certain anthropometric criteria of physical school readiness, namely, changes in proportion of head, arm and leg size, relative to the total body. The head will become smaller, the arms and legs longer; the protrusion of jaw and forehead will change; shoulder width will increase; and body contours will be formed predominantly by muscles and joints and less by subcutaneous fat.

While successful validation of Zeller's criteria has been only sporadic, a systematic study carried out by Meinert (1955) failed to show any relationship between them and measures of school readiness. In a Swedish investigation, correlations between intellectual and social school readiness and scores based on Zeller's indices were conspicuously low (Johansson, 1965). It has been demonstrated, however, that among simple anthropometric data, height is relatively the best predictor of school readiness (Johansson, 1965; Kohen-Raz, 1969; see Table 2). Still, its individual contribution to the predictive validity of a school readiness test battery is not large enough to justify its use as a practical school readiness measure.

A different psychobiological approach to school readiness is represented by investigations based on neurological examinations. Ozer constructed a battery of neurological tests, relatively simple to administer, which have shown predictive and concurrent validity with various criteria of school readiness (Ozer, 1968; Ozer & Deem, 1968).

Ozer's "Measure for Neurological Evaluation of School-Age Children," explicitly defined by the author as "a relevant examination of brain function," can be administered by any adequately trained school physician within 10–15 minutes. It is composed of: (a) "nonmotor"; (b) "motor" and (c) not specifically designated items.

The nonmotor items are discrimination of left and right on own and examiner's body; crossing over of left hand to right ear and vice versa; intelligibility

Table 2
Correlations between Height, Weight, and School Readiness

	Height	Weight
California data (N = 51)[a]		
Kindergarten teacher evaluation	.38**	.21
Arithmetic school readiness		
Counting	.46**	.19
Grouping	.15	.10
Ordinal numbers	.40**	.24
Coordination	07	−.02
Conservation	.23	.13
Arithmetic problems	.26†	.17
Bender Gestalt test	.15	.18
Peabody picture vocabulary	.07	−.13
Swedish Data (N = 235)[b]		
Reading readiness	.11	.05
Mathematics readiness	.20**	.10
Fine motor readiness	.08	.03
Work readiness	.20**	.08
Emotional readiness		
Reaction to others	.16*	.16*
Social readiness		
Attitude to classmates	.02	.03

[a] Data from Kohen-Raz (1969, p. 33).
[b] Data from Johansson (1965, p. 120).
† $p = .1$.
* $p = .05$.
** $p = .01$.

of speech during examination; localization of stimuli applied to face and hand; an auditory distractibility item ("sound–touch"); and a task of visual figure ground discrimination. The group of motor items includes standing on one foot and heel to toe; tapping feet; hopping in place; tapping rhythmically with one foot and ipsilateral finger (this is actually a task of executing a relatively complex synergetic movement); touching own nose and index finger of examiner in alternation; rapid alternating touching of fingertips with thumb of same hand; performing rapid lip and tongue movements on demand. Among the unspecified items we find testing sense of position (up and down); inducing optokinetic nystagmus; discriminating two points by touch; reproducing geometrical forms from tactile impressions.

As can be seen from Table 3, the predictive validity of this neurological school readiness test is satisfactory and compares fairly with an American psychological school readiness battery, the metropolitan readiness test. It will be noted that the "motor" items of the neurological examination correlate with first grade

Table 3

Predictive Validity of Ozer's Neurological School Readiness Examination Compared with Validity of Metropolitan Readiness Test[a]

Sample	School readiness tests given close to school entrance	Stanford achievement battery at end of first grade				Reading level at end of first grade
		Word reading	Vocabulary	Spelling	Arithmetic	
Culturally disadvantaged N = 43	Metropolitan readiness	.33*[b]	.43**	.56**	.67**	.40**
	Ozer's neurological examination "nonmotor"	.26*	.52*	.45**	.41**	.71**
	Ozer's neurological examination "motor"	.11	.22	.01	.12	.10
General population N = 45	Metropolitan readiness	.66**	.60**	.76**	.86**	.74**
	Ozer's neurological examination "nonmotor"	.38**	.70**	.49**	.53**	.54**
	Ozer's neurological examination "motor"	.30**	.31*	.35**	.38**	.33*

[a]From Ozer and Deem (1968).
[b]Numbers are Peason correlation coefficients.
*$p = .05$.
**$p = .01$.

scholastic achievements in a general population sample, but not in a culturally disadvantaged (predominantly black) group. In three instances, the nonmotor part of neurological evaluation predicts scholastic performance better than the metropolitan test, namely, vocabulary in both groups and reading level in the disadvantaged, the latter being especially noteworthy ($r = .71$ compared to $r = .40$). Ozer's tests thus promise to provide valuable insight into psychobiological correlates of school readiness.

Another aspect of the problem is revealed by developmental EEG studies. In spite of the scarcity of investigations in this area, Corbin and Bickford's data (1955, p. 22) seem to suggest that the age of school readiness is a transitional phase characterized by a shift from a preponderance of slow wave activity characteristic of preschool age to a dominance of higher frequencies in age groups 7 and older (see Figure 1). Given the low reliability of EEG records and the large variance between brain maturation levels defined by the EEG within each age group, it is rather doubtful that this technique could be used as a method to assess school readiness. A comparison of EEG patterns in scholastically mature and immature subjects, however, might still be worth undertaking for its theoretical importance.

If the development of psychomotor ability is an indicator of neurophysiologi-

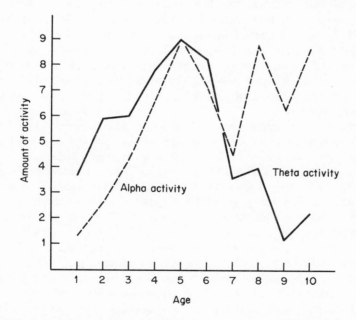

Figure 1 Maturation changes in amount of activity in theta and alpha bands in EEG records at various ages. [From Corbin & Bickford, 1955].

cal maturation, a decisive improvement of certain motor skills in three functional areas should be considered as a possible criterion of psychobiological school readiness. These areas are (a) static balance ability, (b) the ability to suppress synkinetic ("overflowing") movements, and (c) the execution of well coordinated synergetic responses involving simultaneous use of contralateral muscle groups. Measuring these motor functions is important not only because they assess "physical and psychobiological school readiness" (in the sense of gross muscle control, resistance to fatigue, or efficient finger coordination in handwriting) but also because of their relationship to cognitive variables.

Static balance, the increased skill to maintain body equilibrium, should—according to biosemiotic theory—improve the ability to differentiate and discriminate between subject and object. This in turn would facilitate the emancipation of the school child from egocentricity. This process, besides being an obvious factor in the child's social adaptation, is considered by Piaget to be a major determinant of operational thought, characterized by the ability to perceive and evaluate a problem from various aspects independent of the "egocentric" point of view of the observer.

In the light of sensoritonic theory, improved static balance might also lead to greater field independence and to a more flexible sensoritonic equilibrium.* This would supposedly reinforce the suppression of overt motor responses and encourage the generation of "virtual" movements. There should then be positive impact on the development of operational thought in that the imagination of flexible and reversible movements would be facilitated (Kohen-Raz, 1965).

Empirical evidence on the relation between school readiness and static balance ability was presented by Kohen-Raz (1970) who used a specially designed method of electronic ataxiametry. (For a detailed description of the method, see Kohen-Raz, 1969.)

Five ataxiametric scores, as well as a composite score measuring static balance ability, showed substantial correlations with various reading tests, an arithmetic school readiness test, and with the kindergarten teacher's evaluation of intellectual, emotional, and social school readiness (see Tables 4 and 5). Kindergarten girls scored significantly higher on static balance items, indicating that their psychomotor (and possibly neurophysiological) functions mature earlier, a finding in accordance with the well-established fact that girls enter school at a higher "organismic age" than boys.

Results of the ataxiametric study also showed a conspicuously higher correlation between static balance and cognitive school readiness for girls (Table 5).

Whether this indicates that psychobiological factors play a more important role in the attainment of school readiness among girls while social factors may be more important among boys remains an open question in need of further study.

---

*See also Wilson's (1976) findings on the link between postural measures at infancy and intelligence level at age 3 (see page 46).

Table 4

Correlations between Static Balance and Mental Achievements, Both Sexes

Grade	Sample	N	Mental tests	Ataxiametric scores[b]					Composite scores[a]
				OF	NC	MO	RO	RC	
K	A	51	Bender					−28*	
			Teacher evaluation	−26**				−33*	−36** (OF + RC)
			Arithmetic problems	−30**					
			Metropolitan match				−28**	−30**	
			Metropolitan number				−26*		
1	B	47	Stanford word	−24		43***	−31**		−44*** (OF + MO + RO)
			Stanford paragraph	−33**		35**			−44*** (OF + MO + RO)
			Stanford total reading	−37***		30**	26***		−47*** (OF + MO + RO)
1	A	26	Hoyt reading	−29	−36	31			−38** (OF + MO)
2	A	18	Hoyt reading	−48**	−39		−41		−50* (OF + NC + RC)
3	A	21	Hoyt reading	−38				−37	−42* (OF + NC + RC)

[a]Specification of composite score is given in parentheses next to correlation coefficient shown in this column.

[b]As ataxiametric scores OF, NC, RO and RC are measures of *instability*, a *positive* relationship between balance ability and mental achievement is manifest in *negative* correlations.

*p approaches .05.

**p = .05.

***p = .01.

Table 5

Correlations between Static Balance and Mental Achievements, Girls

Grade	Sample	N	Mental tests	Ataxiametric scores					
				OF	NC	MO	RO	RC	Composite scores[a]
K	A	25	Teacher evaluation	-43**					-52** (OF + RC)
			Arithmetic problems						
1	B	23	Metropolitan word			-25	-41**		
			Metropolitan numb.			36*	-42*		
			Metropolitan copy			42**		40**	
			Stanford word	-21		56***	-31		-50** (OF + MO + RO)
			Stanford paragraph	-29		59***	-26		-58*** (OF + MO + RO)
			Stanford total reading number	-28		63***	-34		-59*** (OF + MO + RO)
			Stanford vocabulary				-44**		
1	A	11	Hoyt reading	-15	-37	26	25		-29 (OF + MO)
2	A	9	Hoyt reading	-27	-45	-46			-50 (OF + NC + RC)
3	A	8	Hoyt reading	-94***				-68	-88*** (OF + NC + RC)

[a]Specification of composite score is given in parentheses next to correlation coefficient shown in this column

* p approaches .05

** p = .05

*** p = .01

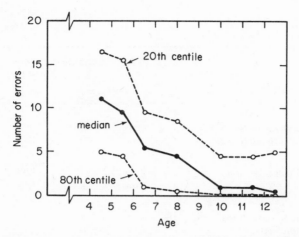

Figure 2 Developmental trends in suppression of synkinetic movement for groups with varying numbers of synkinetic errors per performance in Rey's "finger lifting" test. [Adapted from Rey, 1952, p. 83.]

The respective Ns for each age are

Age	4–4:11	5–5:11	6–6:11	7–8:11	9–10:11	11–11:11	12–12:11
N:	16	18	21	51	86	30	30

Developmental patterns of the ability to suppress synkinetic movements was measured by Rey (1952). His tests show a steep progress between the ages of 5 and 7 (see Figure 2), as well as a conspicuous developmental lag in mentally retarded subjects (1952, p. 90). These data suggest that these motor skills may play an important role in the attainment of school readiness. Decisive improvement in synergetic movement performance at school entrance age is also reflected in Sloan's norms of the Oseretzki scales standardized on American populations (see Table 6; Sloan, 1955).

If sensoritonic and biosemiotic theory are accepted as a basis for a psychobiological model of school readiness, then it may be assumed that improved and differentiated bimanual activity would be another factor promoting the development of operational reasoning. This activity requires the imagination of at least two mutually independent "internalized" movements. Piaget himself has formulated certain assumptions about neurophysiological correlates of reversibility related to internalized action:

> When the nervous activity is no more projected onward (like in the more inferior forms) it must not turn around the same circuits. Therefore there are now simultaneously continuous constructions of new circuits and possibilities of passages from one to the other along all connection paths. From here a reversibility, having become complete, or "aiguillages" [1949, p. 253].

Some experimental evidence about the progress of movement internalization and

Table 6
Development of Complex Synergies[a]

		Percentage of subjects passing item at ages		
Item		5:6–6:5	6:6–7:5	7:6–8:5
Item No. 6				
Tapping rhythmically with feet and finger	Boys	48	66	85
of homolateral hand simultaneously	Girls	30	54	80
Item No. 10				
Close and open hands alternately	Boys	37	49	63
	Girls	38	51	57
Item No. 16				
Tapping with feet and describing circles with	Boys	14	32	35
both hands outstretched	Girls	10	17	37
Item No. 21				
Winding thread while walking	Boys	18	30	40
	Girls	10	32	27

[a]Adapted from Sloan (1955).

its increase at school entrance age has been given by Rey (1949, 1969). He asked subjects ranging in age from 5 to 8 years to draw a square as quickly as possible. They were then instructed to close their eyes and, without moving a limb, "imagine" at maximal speed the drawing movement previously executed. They announced when they had completed the imagined drawing. Children from the ages of 5 to 7 were unable to refrain from moving their arms while imagining the drawing (Rey, 1969, p. 70). Older children, while able to inhibit overt motion of their limbs, still showed lip, jaw, and eyelid movements. Only subjects 8 or older and adults were able to suppress visible external movements completely. It seems (as shown by experiments on silent reading by Edtfeld, 1959) that Rey would probably have also obtained significant electromyographic outputs from involved muscle systems from his completely "immobile" subjects. Comparing the time of execution of the motor performance to the time of the imagined execution, Rey found, contrary to naive expectation, execution took less time than imagination. Further, this difference was greater in adults, and the absolute time of both execution and imagination decreased with age.

Rey draws two conclusions from these studies. First, imagination of movement is vicariously related to its execution. Second, the representation of a movement is more complex than the overt movement response because, according to Rey's assumption, the imagination of movement requires (*a*) inhibition of the external action; (*b*) a more discrete vicarious discharge of motor impulses in a "privileged" motor system (eye muscles, speech apparatus) which in turn must be inhibited in order not to overflow in overt movement; (*c*) control of the "internalized" movement by proprioceptive feedback (1949, p. 222).

It will be noted that Rey's experiments also demonstrate the transition from complete failure to suppress external motion during the imagination of motor activity at kindergarten age to a considerable ability of "movement internalization" or "movement representation" after school entrance.

The hypothesis that there is a linkage between multidirectional movement representations and concrete operational thought was tested by Kohen-Raz. He found substantial correlation between scores on a "movement representation test" and levels of concrete operational reasoning measured by Piaget's clinical method (Kohen-Raz, 1954).

In this context, a paper by Lunzer (1968) should also be mentioned which emphasizes the intrinsic relationship between the ability to reason on the level of concrete operations and the ability to pursue two independent trains of thought. In short, the genesis of "concrete operational thought," can be explained as a function of coordinated, reversible, reality-adapted movement representations. In Piaget's (1949) own words: "The whole evolution of intelligence in the child is characterized by an internalisation of effective actions into actions simply represented, and into operations—these latter being characterized by their reversibility [p. 241]."

It thus appears that the determinants of physical and psychobiological school readiness are not so much physical growth and shifts in body proportions as the result of the following processes:

1. Growth and differentiation of motor-inhibiting mechanisms that cause an increase in movement representations on the principle of sensoritonic vicariousness.
2. Strengthened static coordination, leading to increased stability of an internalized spatial frame of reference, enabling directional differentiation of movement representations and subject—object relationships.
3. The growing ability to suppress synkinetic movements and execute complex and partly antagonistic synergies, presumably contributing, through a process of internalization, to the imagination of coordinated and multidirectional movements.

To review the theoretical outlooks and empirical evidence presented in this chapter, the existence of psychobiological factors in school readiness cannot be denied although their objective measurement at present seems to be possible only indirectly, chiefly through neurological, psychomotor, and ataxiametric indices.

Obviously, more systematic research in this domain is needed to develop a comprehensive theory of psychobiological aspects of school readiness. The development of such a theory seems to be important not only from the point of view of basic research in child development but also in the light of the necessity to improve the school guidance systems responsible for screening and placement of the child at the time of school entrance.

7

Psychobiological Effects
of Birth Season

The effects of season on physiological processes in animals and humans are well known.* Some of them, such as physical growth spurts (Stolz, 1951, p. 418) and the arousal of sexual and migration instincts seem to be the results of seasonal variations in light and temperature which directly affect hormonal processes (Hinde & Steel, 1966). Others, such as seasonal differences in the incidence of congenital malformation (Wehrung & Hay, 1970), dental caries (Sainsburg, 1965), or mental deficiency (Knobloch & Pasamanick, 1958), cannot be explained in such a straightforward way. Although it may be assumed that both the fetus in utero and the neonate are vulnerable to a variety of factors (such as diet of the pregnant mother, virulence of bacteria, radiation, or exposure to air) which are affected in turn by the seasonal cycle, the specific causal linkages between these factors and the various physical effects of birth season remain obscure and in need of clarification.

In the context of the psychobiological aspects of cognitive growth, our interest is focused not on general seasonal or birth season effects on *physiological* processes but on their eventual impact on *cognitive* development. The purpose of investigating this impact is not to discover mental differences between subjects born in different seasons—which, as will be shown, are trivial—but rather (*a*) to provide some indirect evidence about the role of biological determinants in mental growth and (*b*) to clarify some methodological issues concerning birth-season variables in developmental research.

*For a general discussion of the topic see Sargent (1951).

As for the first issue, the mere demonstration of significant differences in mental achievement between populations that differ with respect to season of birth—after all relevant intervening variables have been controlled—would indicate that such differences are likely to be produced by biological factors, largely uncontaminated by the direct intervention of the social environment. This assumption would be strengthened if such seasonal differences persist among older groups (adolescents and adults) among whom the impact of social factors on mental development is supposed to increase. Finally, if birth-season differences in mental scores are absent in infancy and childhood but emerge at adolescence (and eventually remain stable throughout adulthood), such findings would suggest that certain psychobiological determinants of mental growth have "delayed effects" and that prenatal and perinatal circumstances induce changes at later stages of development while leaving earlier phases unaltered. Such a model of delayed impact stands in contrast (but not necessarily in contradiction) to the generally accepted model of cumulative developmental effects which emphasizes early vulnerability and the cumulative, increasingly irreversible effects of early environmental stimulation or traumatization.

As for the methodological aspects of the problem, any consistent appearance of birth-season differences in mental measurements, even if they were not significant within individual samples, would imply that season of birth routinely be controlled in developmental research just as sex and parental background are controlled. The traditional control of age by years would be insufficient because seasonal differences within age groups would be masked. More attention would also have to be paid to the seasonal cutoff points between age groups since mean ages would be likely to vary because of the relative predominance of subjects showing seasonal precocity or retardation within cohorts.

Another methodological issue involves the relative ease of exploring seasonal effects, provided that large samples were available. Once the psychobiological variables suspected to be linked with the seasonal effect were traced or defined in a widely sampled explorative study, a rigorously controlled experiment designed to manipulate these variables could be carried out in the laboratory on a small scale.

Evidence of birth season effects on mental development has been reported in a number of surveys and studies. Pintner and Forlano (1943) compiled the results of 11 different investigations, demonstrating consistent mental superiority among subjects born in the warmer and brighter seasons (see Table 7). Such findings have also been confirmed in two studies carried out in the southern hemisphere where the distribution of solar radiation is inverted (Fitt, 1941; Pintner and Forlano, 1939). In most of the investigations cited, conventional IQ measures were used as criteria of mental performance.

In more recent research (Orme, 1963), significant mental differences, as measured by the Raven matrices (1962), were found within a group of mentally retarded adults (IQ range 40–90) dichotomized by the average seasonal tempera-

Table 7

Birth Season and Intelligence Differences, Summary of Studies[a]

Author	Date	Cases	Lowest		Highest	
			Season	Mean intelligence	Season	Mean intelligence
Blonsky	1929	453 backward children	Autumn	81.3	Spring	84.3
			Winter	81.3		
Pintner	1931	4,925 school children	Winter	95.9	Spring	97.2
					Summer	97.2
Pintner and Forlano	1933	17,502 school children (IQ's 85 to 100)	Winter	100.65	Spring	102.3
Looft	1934	337	Summer	90.3	Spring	91.3
Pintner and Maller	1937	6,353 school children	Winter	94.5	Autumn	96.5
Fialkin and Beckman	1938	3,189 adult men	Winter	6.53*	Spring	6.69*
Pintner and Forlano	1939	2,907 children in southern hemisphere	Winter	101.5	Spring	102.8
			Autumn	101.5		
		8,985 low IQ's	Winter	64.96	Spring	65.5
MacMeeken Held	1939	658 institutional feeble minded	Winter	52.2	Spring	53.2
	1940	874 school children	Spring	99.4	Summer	101.2
Forlano and Ehrlich	1941	2,327 university students	Winter	49.3**	Summer	50.4**
		7,897 college students	Autumn	211.8***	Spring	214.3***
			Winter	211.8***		
Fitt	1941	22,356 children ages 10, 11, 12	Autumn	100.77	Summer	102.27

[a] From Pintner and Forlano (1943, p. 26).

* Sigma units.

** Percentile.

*** Score.

ture of their gestation period. Those whose embryonic development coincided with the warmer seasons had significantly higher quotients. Knobloch and Pasamanick (1958), basing their data on total annual admissions to a state institution for the mentally retarded over a period of 35 years, found a significantly higher incidence of subjects born during the winter. Davies (1964), however, did not find any seasonal variations among normal adults using the Raven matrices, vocabulary tests, and scales of emotional and social adjustment. The fact that her sample of 300 subjects, divided by decades into six age groups, was rather small in part might account for her negative findings.

A different aspect of birth-season effects on intellectual ability and scholastic achievement was recently explored by British investigators. They discovered that (within the British stream system of junior and secondary schools) significantly more pupils born between September and December are placed in the scholastically advanced A and B streams (Sutton, 1967). On the other hand, subjects born between May and August predominate in the lowest level streams (D, E, and F) but subjects born between January and April are in between. These findings contrast sharply with those presented before which showed consistent mental precocity in populations born during the summer. However, as the British authors state, these birth-season effects seem to be environmentally determined by the British law governing school attendance and therefore unrelated to prenatal or perinatal events. Because British children enter junior school on September 1 if they are 7 years old before that date, the subjects born between September and December will be 7:8 to 7:11 years old when they enter junior school, but the subjects born between May and August will be only 7:0 to 7:3 years old. (Obviously, winter subjects will be in between.) In addition, the compulsory British infant school recruits children immediately after their fifth birthdays, but unlike junior school which starts only in September infant school also admits them at the beginning of the spring term. Thus autumn subjects between 5:0 and 5:3 years old in January enter infant school in the spring and profit from a longer period of preschool education ($2\frac{1}{2}$ years) while those who enter infant school in September enjoy only 2 years. Subjects born in the autumn thus have a double advantage: They are the oldest (and presumably the most mentally mature) in the class, and they have also had the most infant school experience.

Although the main issue considered by the British authors was planning alterations of the British educational system to ameliorate the cumulative impact of the "environmental birth season effect," they also report another finding that deserves attention from a psychobiological point of view: Although the scholastic achievement of pupils born during summer are definitely lower than that of the rest of the educational group, their performance on the Eleven Plus examinations is equal to that of the other seasonal groups. This change is also apparent in the disappearance of the "environmental seasonal effect" both at the grammar school level and on the GEC examinations.* Sutton (1967) explains these findings by assuming that the positively selected, more gifted grammar school students are able to overcome the age and schooling deficit induced by the British school admission regulations. We are tempted to speculate, however, that the biological birth season effect reported in other studies may be covertly compensating the "biologically" precocious subjects born in summer for their lag in chronological age and scholastic experience. As will be shown later, the biological birth-season effect seems to have a definite impact on physiological and mental puberty that is possibly more pronounced at this developmental period than during child-hood. This could explain the achievement of the British adolescents born in summer on the Eleven Plus and GEC examinations. It should be noted, however, that the use of the stream system in English secondary schools, which coincides with the beginning of adolescence, is likely to reinforce the "environmental birth season effect" by placing low achievers in low-achieving streams and thereby suppressing the pubertal "biological" precocity of students predominantly born in the summer.

In recent investigations of physiological maturation and mental growth during adolescence carried out in Israel (Kohen-Raz, 1974), the mental precocity of middle class, summer-born girls was demonstrated.† They were shown to per-form significantly better, chiefly on verbal analogies but also on vocabulary, sentence completion, concept formation, and the Guttman–Schlesinger analyti-cal test of visuo-spatial matrices (Guttman & Schlesinger, 1966). The birth-season effect was most pronounced among eighth graders (chronological age 14 years) and gradually decreased among the lower age groups, being almost absent among fifth graders (age 11). On numerical tests, however, only among ninth graders (age 15) was some marginally significant seasonal effect observable. This general pattern paralleled the distribution of seasonal effects on height and weight which was found entirely in the physical precocity of female summer-born subjects at the seventh and eighth grade levels.

Among pubertal males from the middle class no statistically significant effect of birth season on mental or physical development was found, except for certain trends that could have been caused by sampling error.

With culturally disadvantaged adolescents, seasonal effects on mental develop-ment appeared only among the oldest age groups (14 years) in both boys and girls (Kohen-Raz, 1973). Such effects were absent from both sexes at the sixth and seventh grade level. The impact of season on intellectual performance was not paralleled by trends in height and weight differences among the disadvan-taged.

It must be emphasized that the samples used in these two studies were considerably smaller than those reported upon by Pintner (1943). The different

*See Armstrong (1966) and Jackson (1964).
†The study is described in greater detail in Chapter 9.

pubertal patterns (seasonal peak effects at age 14) do not contradict the findings of the larger investigation presented in Pintner's survey. The latter did not explicitly consider adolescent populations and did not take into consideration eventual age, grade, and sex differences.

A different aspect of the phenomenon is the effect of birth season on menarcheal age. In both middle class and culturally disadvantaged girls born during the summer season (July to December) in Israel, menarche tends to occur earlier, as shown in Table 8 (Kohen-Raz, 1974).*

Other birth-season effects on *physical* development were recently reported in three French studies by Jeurrisen (1970), Benech (1970), and Pineau (1970). Jeurrisen found a significant relationship between season of birth and season of menarche, in that significantly more girls' menarches occurred within 2 months of the month of their birthday. Menarcheal dates within his sample were not randomly distributed throughout the months of the year but showed peaks in January, May, and December and lowest incidence in March, June, and October.

Benech found seasonal fluctuations in birth weight, correlations between birth weight and pubertal stature and weight, and seasonal variations in preadolescent physical growth in boys. The seasonal differences coincided with those found in the other studies: The summer-born subjects were precocious.

In Pineau's study, negative correlations between temperature at period of conception and birth weight were reported, while the latter was positively related to the average monthly temperature of the five final months of gestation. In groups of 13-year-old girls, Pineau found a positive relationship between birth weight and pubertal physical growth and a significantly higher incidence of premenarcheal girls with low birth weight (thus cross-validating Benech's findings in a female sample). He also found mental precocity on verbal tests in prepubertal girls with higher birth weights. Although not directly relevant, Wiener's findings should be cited in this context. They showed significantly lower WISC scores among 8-10-year-old children whose birth weights were below 2500 gm and whose gestation periods were less than 38 weeks (Wiener, 1970).

Although the French studies demonstrate no direct relationship between

---

*Different statistical techniques have been employed to demonstrate this seasonal influence (Kohen-Raz, 1974). Some caution, however, has to be taken not to contaminate the results with so-called "age grade ceiling effects." On any assessment of the relationship between chronological and menarcheal age in age groups including a considerable proportion of premenarcheal subjects, the chronologically older part of such a group will contain more girls with higher menarcheal age simply because in the younger part of the group the subjects maturing later will be still premenarcheal and thus excluded from the sample. This might result in a spurious positive relationship between chronological and menarcheal age. This ceiling effect can be controlled by matching pairs of early and late maturing girls closely by chronological age or by excluding from the group investigated all subjects whose menarcheal age is above the chronological age of the youngest subject at the date of menarcheal age assessment.

Table 8
Relationship between Season of Birth and Menarcheal Age, Israeli Samples

Middle class, grades 6, 7, and 8 combined		
Menarcheal age	Winter	Summer
12:9 and older	50	39
12:8 and younger	28	42

$$N = 159$$
$$\chi^2 = 4.57$$
$$p < .05$$

Culturally disadvantaged[a]				
Grade		n	Mean menarcheal age (months)	SD
6	Summer	24	143.3	6.56
	Winter	25	147.8	6.42
7	Summer	31	152.6	10.03
	Winter	47	154.8	10.57
8	Summer	17	151.6	7.52
	Winter	18	148.6	10.61

[a]F between seasonal groups 2.83, $p = .1$.

season of birth and menarcheal age or between season of birth and mental development, the data suggest the possibility of the following linkages: Birth during the summer period seems to be associated with higher birth weight, precocious pubertal physical development, earlier menarche in girls, and mental precocity (on verbal tests) in premenarcheal girls.

These birth-season effects on pubertal physical growth and menarcheal age do not seem to be related directly to the problem of psychobiological correlates of cognitive growth. But it will be shown in the next chapter that pubertal precocity correlates with mental superiority. It therefore may be suspected that a common psychobiological factor linked with birth season may be the cause of both earlier menarche and precocious mental development in girls.

Because they do not appear until puberty, the effects of birth season on mental development may be of the "delayed" type—an early influence on later development (see page 81). It also seems that the impact of seasonal factors on mental development during adolescence is stronger in girls than in boys (Kohen-Raz, 1974), a phenomenon that needs to be explored. Given our present state of knowledge, we are unable to offer any plausible theoretical explanation.

Pintner and Forlano (1943) describe the subject of their survey as "a problem which seemed at first ridiculous and inconsequential." In the light of recent advances in biology and genetics, however, supported by evidence from animal studies, and in view of the growing readiness of behavioral scientists to accept biological principles and models, explorations of birth-season effects are no longer a strange and far-fetched research objective. Pintner and Forlano, trying to systematize the various ad hoc explanations and hypotheses presented by the authors cited in their survey, propose a dichotomy of "exogenous" and "endogenous" theories. According to the "exogenous" explanations, the main causes of the birth-season effect are changes in temperature and sunshine which in turn are believed to influence the health and vitality of mother and child decisively. According to Pintner and Forlano, these assumptions are supported by the well-established fact of different birth rates among different groups of people at different seasons of the year. In line with this hypothesis, Pintner and Forlano report Spearman correlations of .59 and .67 between IQ, monthly sunshine, and monthly temperature.

The higher mortality in winter periods also tends to substantiate the temperature–light–health hypothesis, except that it might be argued that the elimination of the less viable (and presumably mentally weaker) winter subjects should cause a rise in IQ among winter groups—which is not the case.

Another remarkable argument presented by proponents of the exogenous theory is the suggestion that selective birth control is practiced predominantly by the middle class, who supposedly prefer to raise babies in the more convenient summer period. Thus in any general population, summer-born groups would include a greater percentage of subjects of higher SES, whose IQs are known to be higher. The mental precocity of summer subjects would therefore appear in samples randomly recruited from general populations of mixed SES. There is ample evidence, however, from studies cited by Pintner and Forlano, from the two Israeli studies (Kohen-Raz, 1974), and from the large-scale investigation by Knobloch and Pasamanick already cited (1958) that birth season effects are not dependent on SES. The "birth control" hypothesis of seasonal effects thus seems to be untenable.

Finally, school entrance schedules and policies have been considered sporadically as possible spurious "exogenous" causes of birth-season differences in mental capability between pupils. We have already discussed the environmental birth season effects caused by school entrance regulations in Britain. In countries where children enter school in the September following their sixth birthday (as in Israel), many parents may tacitly or openly encourage gifted children born in October, November, or December (months considered to belong to the summer period in the Israeli studies) to enter first grade in September, before their sixth birthday. Other parents may postpone the school entrance of a slow learner or mentally borderline case of same chronological age for an entire year. Such children, who are 1 year older than the educational year of their classmates, would be excluded from data analyses because it is customary to control chronological age within age–grade groups. Thus a positive selection of bright pupils would be left in the younger, summer born part of the sample. Although it is plausible that parents are able to estimate the scholastic ability of their children, it is hard to see how they could predict the menarcheal age of their daughters, which has also been shown to be affected by birth season.

Some explanations might be considered midway between exogenous and endogenous—those which consider the birth-season effect to be a result of metabolic changes produced by temperature changes during the gestation period (Mills, 1941; Orme, 1963).

An intriguing endogenous hypothesis was formulated by Fitt (1941). He assumes that some remnants of seasonal physiological rhythms may persist in humans analogous to those that induce hibernation in some animals. Consequently, Fitt argues, a human fetus conceived just before or during the winter period (the period of hibernation) would profit from a quieter intrauterine metabolism, which in turn influence the growth of the nervous system favorably, during the critical stages of the first two months of pregnancy. Obviously, winter conception results in late summer birth, which would explain the mental precocity of the summer born individual.

Fitt's (1941) hypothesis that the embryogenesis of the nervous system during the first 12 weeks of gestation rather than time of birth might be the critical growth period affected by seasonal factors was tested by Knobloch and Pasmainck in 1958. But while Fitt tried to explain the mental superiority of summer-born (winter-conceived) subjects by assuming greater intrauterine tranquility during the winter season, Knobloch and Pasamanick suspected that metabolic deficiencies (caused by a presumed inadequate diet of the pregnant mother early in pregnancy during the hot summer months) caused a higher incidence of mentally retarded children born in winter. Using the average admissions to a state institution for the retarded for a 35-year period as the source of their data, they were unable to confirm this hypothesis. Among other evidence disproving the hypothesis, it was shown that no significant differences in the estimated birth rate of retardates could be found between years of economic depression (including the year 1929) and years of economic boom, despite the documented contrast in nutritional conditions between these periods. Knobloch and Pasamanick, however, succeeded in isolating temperature at a time of birth as the critical seasonal factor. Their extensive time sampling enabled them to use average summer temperatures during 35 successive years as the independent variable and to relate them to the corresponding annual intake of retardates. In accordance with results of the other studies cited before, the incidence of mental retardation was highest during the years with the lowest summer temperatures.

Although none of the theories presented here, whether exogenous or endogenous, seems to be satisfactory, promising discoveries in the field of biogenetics may shed new light on the issue. In a recent investigation of the effect of hormones on DNA synthesis and cell numbers in developing animal brains (in this case, chicks and rats) (Zamenhof, Marthens, & Bursztyn, 1971), it was incidentally found that the amount of brain DNA in newborn chicks and rats varies strikingly with seasonal variations in daylight. The hormone believed to mediate this seasonal effect is thyroxine. Because the relationship of DNA quantity to mental and physical growth is presently being intensively investigated, this study may help lead to an explanation of the seasonal influence on cognitive growth and justify the exploration of birth-season effects as an approach to psychobiological aspects of cognitive functioning.

8

Physiological Maturation and Mental Growth during Preadolescence and Puberty

It is well documented from observation and research that the pubertal activity of the gonads is preceded by an increase in body growth generally described as "the adolescent growth spurt." According to both experimental evidence and theoretical considerations summarized by Tanner (1962), it is also assumed that this growth spurt and the incidence of puberty in general are related to brain maturation, in that an unknown maturational status of the central nervous system precipitates the hormonal changes that induce puberty. Given the intimate relationship between intensified body growth and pubertal maturation, both controlled by the brain, it is also plausible to propose the hypothesis that mental growth, which is also based on the maturation of the nervous system, could be related to physiological puberty. This could occur in two ways: (*a*) early occurrence of puberty could be an expression of accelerated brain maturation and be linked with mental precocity or (*b*) intensified physical growth at the threshold of adolescence could be paralleled by a simultaneous spurt in mental maturation. Both hypotheses have attracted various investigators during the past 40 years (Anastasi, 1958; Jones & Conrad, 1944; Kuhlen, 1952; Tanner, 1962; Terman & Merrill, 1937; Thurston & Ackerson, 1929; Abernethy, 1936).

An exhaustive overview of past research and recent opinions of investigators summarized by Ljung (1965, pp. 7–15) and Tanner (1962, p. 208) lead to the conclusion that the occurrence of a pubertal mental growth spurt is rather doubtful. Substantial evidence of a general relationship between physical and mental precocity, however, was corroborated in two large-scale British studies (Douglas & Ross, 1964; Nisbet & Illsley, 1963). The findings unanimously indicate that boys and girls with earlier puberty are mentally precocious not only at adolescence but also in late childhood. Nevertheless, there is some controversy about the continuity of this mental superiority during postadolescence. Douglas and Ross demonstrated significantly higher cognitive test scores continuing among such boys and girls as old as 15, but Nisbet's data present contrary evidence. Neither of the studies investigated the occurrence of an adolescent mental growth spurt.

Ljung (1965) used data derived from the entire Swedish elementary school population born on the fifteenth of each month. These children were given scholastic achievement tests during the third, fourth, sixth, and eighth grades. Ljung interprets the significant cross-sectional monthly increase in mental scores within age groups as evidence of mental growth spurts which typically occur during the sixth grade among girls and during the eighth grade among boys. Ljung relies heavily on the time discrepancy between the occurrence of the mental growth spurt in the two sexes as proof of their relatedness to physiological puberty. Because his design did not include physiological measurements as independent variables, however, his claim to have traced an adolescent spurt in mental growth is considerably weakened.

Epstein (1974) attempted to demonstrate regular biennial growth spurts in the human brain (measurable by developmental changes in skull circumference) that seem to be associated with mental growth spurts which were assessed cross-sectionally and longitudinally with routine mental tests. Epstein's investigations were based on extensive surveys and data analysis of studies in the area of neurophysiology, anatomy, and educational and developmental psychology. According to the evidence presented, one of the mental and physical growth spurts occurs between the ages of 10 and 12, and corresponds roughly to the prepubertal physical growth spurt of girls. With boys, however, this spurt occurs about one year later. Because this study is based on a reelaboration of data not originally gathered for the purpose of investigating growth spurts, it is of limited value. Likewise, if physical growth spurts are related to mental growth acceleration, sex differences should appear, especially during the prepubertal period when the later occurrence of the male physical growth spurt is an undisputable fact. Nevertheless, Epstein's work makes a substantial contribution to the exploration of psychobiological aspects of cognitive growth in general and of the problems of adolescent mental growth in particular.

Another attempt to examine the general relationship between physiological and mental maturation, and to explore the eventual occurrence of a pubertal mental growth spurt was made in three studies (designated I, II, and III). All three studies, which are described in detail in this chapter, were carried out in Israel between 1967 and 1972.

The samples used in the investigations were selected from preadolescents and adolescents of both sexes enrolled in the four upper grades (5, 6, 7, and 8) of elementary school, their mean ages at the beginning of the scholastic year being 11, 12, 13, and 14 years.* The samples, described in detail in the following section, were recruited from the upper middle and lower middle classes in studies I and II and from lower class, culturally disadvantaged homes in study III.

In all the three studies, the following hypotheses were tested:

1. If a general relationship exists between physiological maturation and mental growth, subjects in more advanced stages of pubertal maturation will score significantly higher on specific mental tests, when age, level of intelligence, ethnic origin, and parental occupation are controlled.

2. If, in addition, a mental growth spurt linked to pubertal growth acceleration does occur, differences between earlier and later maturing subjects (or correlations between their mental and physiological measurements) should be more pronounced when the subjects compared are approaching or undergoing their pubertal physical growth spurts, but these differences or correlations should be smaller or eventually disappear when earlier and later maturers are tested before or after that developmental phase.

The disadvantaged adolescents used in study III were also exposed to a structured training program in higher forms of reasoning. Consequently, two additional hypotheses were examined in this study:

3. Culturally disadvantaged adolescents can be trained in higher forms of reasoning.

4. Experimental effects are eventually affected by pubertal physiological maturation, so that an interaction between maturational and training effects can be demonstrated.

SAMPLES

Table 9 lists the samples used in the three studies by sex and socioeconomic status. It will be noted that study I, which was a pilot project, included only girls. The sample used in study III, designed to demonstrate training effects, had to be separated into experimental and control groups and is therefore the largest.

All pupils whose chronological ages were above or below those of their grade level were excluded, thus all those suspected of mental precocity or retardation

---

*The Israeli compulsory elementary school system consisted—at the time the studies were carried out—of eight grades. All children born during a given calendar year enter the first grade on September first of their sixth year after their birth, their age range thus being 5:9 to 6:8 on school entrance day.

Table 9
Samples Used in Three Studies

| | Boys | | | | | Girls | | | | |
| | 1 | | 2 | | 3 | 1 | | 2 | | 3 |
Study Grade	Upper middle class	Lower middle class	Upper middle class	Lower middle class	Disadvantaged	Upper middle class	Lower middle class	Upper middle class	Lower middle class	Disadvantaged
5	—	—	40	66	—	—	—	39	55	—
6	—	—	41	50	127	39	19	42	55	141
7	—	—	32	46	122	43	24	34	45	117
8	—	—	37	37	120	42	11	35	46	122

were eliminated. In the disadvantaged population of study III however, the number of pupils one year older than others at their grade level turned out to be 10% to 25% of the classroom population. These students, who entered school late or eventually repeated a grade, were suspected of being intellectually and physically inferior to their classmates and therefore deserving of special attention in the light of the linkage between mental and physical development under investigation. Consequently, they were retained in the study but were treated as a separate subgroup for purposes of data elaboration.

METHOD

Measurement of Physical Development

Physical measurements including height and weight, were assessed six times during the 2-year periods of the studies, in December, March, and June of each year. These examinations were carried out by registered school nurses. The nurses also questioned the girls about their menarche and assessed their menarcheal age. In boys, the growth of pubic hair was examined by physicians at their schools using Tanner's criteria (Tanner, 1962), and observer reliability was established by having the head nurse and the physician examine an auxiliary sample. (Observer agreement was 90%.) Pubic hair examinations were made twice, at the end of each of the two scholastic years.

Measurement of Mental Development

A battery of 11 group tests was administered four times, at the beginning (November) and at the end (June) of the two scholastic periods. These tests were supposed to measure "formal reasoning"* in three areas, numerical, verbal, and perceptual–spatial.

Lunzer (1965) showed that analogy tests with "directional distractors" are valid indicators of the ability to reason formally. Accordingly, one test of numerical analogies and two tests of verbal analogies were constructed. In the

---

*Formal reasoning has been defined operationally by Lunzer (1965) as the mental capacity to form and understand second order relationships in the sense of performing reversible operations with complex cognitive units which themselves are relations, classifications, seriations, etc. One of the characteristics of formal operational thought is its power to transcend the limits of empirical facts and findings and to conceptualize knowledge within a superordinated system of hypothetical and deductive reasoning, which makes possible the prediction of facts and situations not yet experienced or never to be experienced.

According to Inhelder and Piaget (1959), the ability of formal reasoning develops decisively at ages 11–13, a period roughly parallel to the adolescent growth spurt. It was thus assumed that the eventual impact of physical pubertal maturation on mental development might be most pronounced on tests measuring this cognitive ability.

verbal area, two tests of deductive reasoning like those originally designed by Donaldson (1963) were added. Raven's matrices (1962) and Guttman and Schlesinger's new "Analytical Test" (GSAT, Guttman & Schlesinger, 1966, 1967)* were considered to examine the ability to solve complex *spatial* analogies. Finally, four subsets of the MILTA (Ortar, 1965), vocabulary, sentence completion, MILTA analogies, and concept formation, recently standardized in Israel, were used. All tests, except Raven's matrices, have parallel forms which were used at the retest. (For detailed description of the tests, their reliability, validity, and administration, see Kohen-Raz, 1969.)

Control of Intervening Variables

Parental ethnic and educational history were controlled in part by treating schools in different SES areas separately. In a similar manner, age, sex, and scholastic experience were controlled by computing separate correlations between mental and physiological measurements within each age–grade–sex subgroup. In addition, these intervening variables were controlled more strictly by reelaborating data by matched-pair techniques. Birth season turned out to be an additional intervening variable (see Chapter 7). It was controlled either by separating seasonal groups within grades or by matching subjects by birth date within 2 months' distance.

Data Elaboration to Test Hypotheses 1 and 2

Hypothesis 1 was tested by assessing overall relationships between physiological and mental variables by means of correlational techniques. The results were cross validated by measuring mental differences between pairs of early and late maturing partners matched for chronological age, scholastic experience, and parental education, applying t tests for correlated means, and using the nonparametric Wilcoxon Test (Siegel, 1956). In order to examine hypothesis 2 (incidence of mental growth spurt linked with pubertal physical growth acceleration), the significance levels, sizes, and direction of correlations (or differences in the matched pairs), were compared across the age–grade–sex groups.

An additional attempt to test hypothesis 2 was made by a method of comparison of physiological maturation constellations." Body growth curves over the 2-year period, eventually revealing peak height velocity, were plotted also showing the incidence of menarche and stages of pubic hair development. On the same graph, the dates of the four mental examinations were inserted. It

---

*This test is similar in principle to the Raven matrices; however, the patterns used are much more complex, and distractors (characterized by rich variation in directionality) have been carefully and systematically constructed.

was thus possible to define the pubertal growth stage attained by each subject at each mental examination and consequently to designate pairs of later and earlier maturing partners matched as already described. These pairs formed three specifiable physiological maturation constellations at mental testing dates:

1. Constellation A: both partners are before their adolescent growth spurt.
2. Constellation B: one partner is at the peak or closely after the growth spurt and the other one still before it or still passing it.
3. Constellation C: both partners pubertal after the growth spurt.

It was hoped the cross-sectional and longitudinal comparisons of the size and significance level of the mental differences occurring in these maturation constellations would provide insight into the critical phases during which physiological maturation discrepancies would produce pronounced mental precocity in earlier-maturing partners. (For details of the method, see Kohen-Raz, 1969b, p. 20.)

Method of Training and Assessment of Training Effects (Hypotheses 3 and 4)

In study III, the sample was subdivided into experimental, placebo-training, and distant control groups. Experimental groups were given structured and graded learning units in formal reasoning and concept formation presented in the form of paper-and-pencil tasks to be performed in two regular lessons per week for a 6–7 month period. Placebo-training groups were formally treated in the same manner, but the learning tasks required no formal reasoning and problem solving but verbal fluency, creative imagination, and application of routine classroom experience instead. Experimental and placebo-training groups were formed by splitting classrooms into two halves matched for IQ. Distant controls did not receive any experimental treatment whatsoever. During the 2-year period of the study, experimental and placebo training were subsequently given to two different subgroups. The subgroup trained during the second year served as additional distant control population during the first year, and training effects (besides being measurable within the trained groups by comparison of pre- and posttraining tests), could be crossvalidated by replication. (For details of the design and training method, see Kohen-Raz, 1973.)

To test hypothesis 3, training effects in the experimental and control groups were assessed by F-tests on the results of the first retest using the scores of the first examination (pretest) as covariant.

In order to examine the interaction between tutoring and physiological maturation (hypothesis 4), analysis of variance was carried out separately for the two sexes, introducing the factor of physiological maturation by dichotomizing each age–grade level by the median of menarcheal age in girls and the median of height as well as of pubic hair growth in boys.* This resulted in the formation of subgroups of earlier and later maturing subjects. Subsequently, the analysis of variance was based on two factors, treatment and maturational levels using the same covariates as before.

RESULTS

Comparison of Mental and Physical Development in Middle Class and Disadvantaged Adolescents

Between the upper and lower middle class groups (I and II) no overall significant mental and physical differences were found. Upper middle class pupils scored consistently higher on all mental tests, and only at age 14 did they significantly surpass lower middle class pupils in height and weight. (Data not tabulated. For details, see Kohen-Raz, 1969a, pp. 109–111). On the other hand, as shown in Tables 10 and 11, culturally disadvantaged adolescents showed a consistent and significant mental and physical inferiority to the middle class pupils of the same age. (In all comparisons with the disadvantaged shown in Tables 10 and 11, upper and lower middle class groups were combined.) Furthermore, the "retarded" disadvantaged (who were one year older than others at their grade level because of repeating a grade or entering school later), were retarded even in comparison to the "regular" disadvantaged. The discrepancy between the mental scores of these two disadvantaged subgroups is significant at the .001 level, and the lag in physical development is conspicuous but not significant.

An inspection of background data revealed that the retarded disadvantaged did not differ from the regular disadvantaged population in ethnic background, parental occupation, or father's education. They did tend to have mothers with less education level, some of whom had not completed elementary school. In any case, these data indicate that regular and retarded disadvantaged adolescents are retarded not only in mental development but also in physical growth. No follow-up data are yet available, so it remains an open question whether they will reach the height and weight of the nondisadvantaged as adults.

The great discrepancy in weight and height between the middle class and retarded disadvantaged (approximating mean differences of 10 kg and 10 cm) cannot be attributed to food deprivation under adverse socioeconomic conditions. To the best of our knowledge, undernourishment in Israel is largely prevented by health and welfare services. It must be assumed that genetic and biological factors are involved in the disadvantaged adolescent's intellectual and physical retardation. Socioeconomic stress may have seriously impeded bio-

---

*A five-point scale proposed by Tanner (1962) was used as measure of pubic hair growth.

Table 10

Comparison of Mental Achievement and Physical Growth in Middle Class and Disadvantaged Adolescents, Boys[a]

Age group	12			13			14		
Socioeconomic Group	A	B	C	A	B	C	A	B	C
N (Range)	73–85	83–89	—	62–67	77–82	23–26	54–73	51–53	24–26
Numerical analogies	18.3	14.6**	—	20.1	19.7	12.9***	23.2	22.7	12.8***
Verbal analogies I	15.3	9.9***	—	18.2	12.6***	7.1***	20.1	14.6***	8.9***
Raven	31.8	22.5***	—	33.5	27.5***	19.2***	35.5	31.4**	24.6**
Height (m)	145.9	142.3	—	151.0	148.4	146.5(*)	159.8	155.6	153.7(**)
Weight (kg)	38.3	35.1	—	45.0	39.8	36.0(***)	49.9	45.5	43.3(***)

[a] Level of significance of t test relative to adjacent left column. Asterisks in brackets indicate significance level relative to column A of same age. Tabulated data are mean scores.

A = Middle class, upper and lower level combined.

B = Disadvantaged regular pupils.

C = Disadvantaged retarded pupils.

* $p = .05$.

** $p = .01$.

*** $p = .001$.

Table 11

Comparison of Mental Achievement and Physical Growth in Middle Class and Disadvantaged Adolescents, Girls[a]

Age group	12			13			14		
Socioeconomic Group	A	B	C	A	B	C	A	B	C
N (Range)	85–92	104–111	—	71–75	75–85	14–15	61–73	51–57	18–20
Numerical Analogies	15.8	13.7	—	18.1	17.3	9.4***	22.0	23.0	14.7***
Verbal analogies I	14.4	10.3***	—	17.7	12.2***	9.0*	19.1	15.3***	9.7***
Raven	29.6	22.4***	—	35.1	26.0***	18.9**	37.7	32.4***	24.7***
Height (m)	145.1	145.0	—	157.3	150.0***	146.7(***)	156.7	154.4	149.2**
Weight (kg)	38.6	37.2	—	44.0	42.5	39.4(*)	49.9	46.7	40.2**

[a]Level of significance of t test relative to adjacent left column. Asterisks in brackets indicate significance level relative to column A of same age.

A = Middle class, upper and lower level combined.

B = Disadvantaged regular pupils.

C = Disadvantaged retarded pupils.

*p = .05.

**p = .01.

***p = .001.

Table 12
Comparison of Menarcheal Age in Middle Class, Disadvantaged, and Retarded Disadvantaged Girls

Age group	12			13			14		
SES	MC	DIS	RET	MC	DIS	RET	MC	DIS	RET
N	43	55	—	63	80	12	61	38	21
Mean menarcheal age	12:12	12:12	—	12:11	12:11	12:10	13:10	12:7	13:7

logical growth in very early, possibly prenatal phases of development, which would accord with recent theories of the biosocial etiology of cultural deprivation (Willerman, 1972).

Menarcheal age does not seem to be related to the delay in height and weight development.* Except for the group of 14-year-old retarded girls, there was no difference in menarcheal age between the groups of disadvantaged and middle class subjects at the same age (Table 12).

Relationship between Physiological Maturation and Mental Achievement in Girls

Relationship between Height and Mental Scores

In both study I and study II, height tended to be significantly related to mental achievement only in the upper middle class groups. Among the premenarcheal girls of study I, it correlated with Raven matrices, concept formation, and MILTA analogies in the sixth and seventh grades but not in the eighth. In study II, among combined groups of pre- and postmenarcheal upper middle class subjects, height correlated positively with deductive reasoning and sentence completion at the sixth grade level, with no test whatsoever at the seventh, and negatively with numerical analogies, concept formation, and Raven matrices at the eighth. (All correlations cited were significant at the .05 level. See Table 13.)

Comparison of matched pairs of the same population demonstrated significantly higher ($p = .05$) mental scores among taller girls on the Raven matices and sentence completion tests at the fifth grade level, on the Raven, verbal

*Considering the evident weight differences between the two groups and assuming that weight and menarcheal age are randomly distributed in the postmenarcheal group at age 14, these findings do not support the hypothesis of the "critical body weight at menarche" proposed by Frisch and Revelle (1970). On the basis of evidence from various sources, this hypothesis was recently rejected at the Paris symposium on puberty, 1974 (Berenberg, 1975).

Table 13
Relationship between Height and Mental Scores, Girls[a]

Grade–age	Socioeconomic level	N	Nonverbal			Verbal				
			Numerical Analogies	Raven	GSAT	Verbal analogies I	Verbal Analogies II	Deductive reasoning	Vocabulary	Sentence completion
6 (12)	Upper middle class	41						+36*		+38*
	Lower middle class	50								
	Disadvant.	92–97								
7 (13)	Upper middle class	32								
	Lower middle class	46		+22*						
	Disadvantaged	77–86				–27				+30
	Retarded	12–14								
8 (14)	Upper middle class	37	–37*							
	Lower middle class	37			–34*					
	Disadvantaged	21–27					–31	–32	–44*	–49*
	Retarded	17–19	+37	+27				+42	+26	+21

[a] Data are Spearman rank correlation coefficients.
* $p = .05$.

Analogies; II and GSA tests at the sixth, marginal superiority (p - .1) on the Raven and GSA tests at the seventh and no relationship (with a tendency to insignificant *inversion*) at the eighth. (Data not tabulated.)

A similar pattern appears in the sample of disadvantaged girls (study III). After an isolated significant positive correlation between height and the Raven test at the seventh grade level, significant inverted relationships show up the eighth (Table 13). This inversion, however, does not appear among the retarded disadvantaged girls whose correlations remain positive but insignificant, possibly because of the small size of the sample. In view of the delayed menarcheal age of this group (see Table 12) and assuming that positive relationships between height and mental scores disappear as menarche approaches, this phenomenon may indicate the general lag in mental and physical development of this group.

These results, besides supporting hypothesis 1, also seem to support hypothesis 2. The relationship between height and mental achievement typically appears in grades five, six, and seven (when the majority of subjects are still in their preadolescent growth spurt) and vanishes or inverts at grade eight (when 90% have passed it). Although the disappearance of this relationship could be caused by the restriction of range resulting from the physical growth deceleration around and after menarche, this would not account for the inversions, as will be discussed later.

Correlations * between Menarcheal Age and Mental Scores * *

In the upper middle class sample of the first study, menarcheal age*** was found to correlate negatively and significantly (p = .05) with the Raven test (ρ = −.65, N = 13) and marginally significantly (p = .1) with MILTA analogies (ρ = −.44, N = 12) in the combined group of sixth and seventh graders. No relationship was found at the eighth grade. In the lower middle class groups of the first study, menarcheal age and mental scores were unrelated.

In the sample of study II, both upper and lower middle class subjects showed similar relationships between menarcheal age and mental achievements during the sixth and seventh grades but discrepant patterns during the eighth grade. Therefore data on all middle class sixth and seventh graders are combined in

---

*The results obtained from the matched pairs technique are similar to those in this section and will not be reported here. The interested reader is referred to the original material (Kohen-Raz, 1969).

**The positive relationship between pubertal maturation and mental achievements predicted by hypothesis 1 is supposed to show significant *negative* correlation between menarcheal age and mental scores.

***It turned out that correlations between mental scores and chronological age in months within age–grade cohorts were generally close to zero (Kohen-Raz, 1974). Therefore, partialling out of chronological age does not produce any sizable changes in the correlations between pubertal maturation and mental scores shown in Table 14.

Table 14

Relationship between Menarcheal Age and Mental Development[a]

Grade–age	Socioeconomic group	N	Nonverbal			Verbal				
			Numerical analogies	Raven	GSAT	Verbal analogies I	Verbal analogies II	Deductive reasoning	Vocabulary	Sentence completion
6 (12)	Middle class	43	−30†	−33*		−48*	−41*	−43*	−27†	−28*
	Disadvantaged	48–52				−28*	−32*	−24†	−25	−39*
	Retarded	—								
7 (13)	Middle class	63								
	Disadvantaged	70–78	+27	+22					+33	
	Retarded	10–12						−23		
8 (14)	Upper middle class	34				+49*		+37*		
	Lower middle class	24	−24		−40*				−39*	
	Disadvantaged	30–36	+33*			+35†				
	Retarded	13–14	−44†	−30		−29	−28	−44†	−38	−31

[a] Data are Spearman rank correlation coefficients.

† $p = .1$.

* $p = .05$.

Table 14, but they are presented separately for eighth graders. It can be seen that pronounced relationships between physiological and mental maturation appear in the sixth grade groups that are entirely absent in the seventh. Although lower middle class eighth graders show correlations in the expected directions between menarcheal age and numerical analogies, GSAT, and vocabulary, zero correlations and even a tendency to inverted relationships (in verbal analogies and deductive reasoning) appear in the upper middle class sample (Table 14).

The pattern of relationships between menarcheal age and mental achievement among disadvantaged girls is similar to that found in the middle class samples. At the sixth grade level (age 12), correlations are significantly negative, indicating a positive relationship between physiological and mental maturation. At the seventh grade level, the relationship vanishes, and at the eighth (age 14) it tends to invert.

The subgroups of retarded girls show a somewhat different pattern (Table 14). The positive relationship between physiological and mental development that disappears among the older upper middle class and regular disadvantaged girls persists at age 14. This pattern is similar to that of the lower middle class subjects.

Relationships between Physiological Maturation and Mental Achievements in Boys

In boys, height and stage of pubic hair growth were used as criteria of physiological maturation.*

Correlation techniques showed a significant relationship between height and numerical analogies, verbal analogies, and vocabulary among the upper middle class eighth graders (Table 15). In contrast, in the lower middle class sample, height correlated significantly with verbal analogies ($r = .34$), deductive reasoning ($r = .28$), and vocabulary ($r = .30$) at the fifth grade level (data not tabulated), and with deductive reasoning, vocabulary, concept formation, and GSAT (also significantly) at the sixth (i.e., during the prepubertal period), but no relationship appeared at the near pubertal and pubertal phases of the seventh and eighth grades (Table 15).

In the samples of regular and retarded disadvantaged boys, height and mental scores correlated consistently at the seventh and eighth grade levels (Table 15). The overall impression obtained from Table 15 is that there is a definite

---

*Obviously, height and pubic hair growth are less reliable criteria of male physiological maturation than menarcheal age in girls. In an attempt to overcome these limitations to a certain extent, (a) the relationships between both pubic hair and height and the mental variables were analyzed separately and crosschecked with both parametric and nonparametric techniques, and (b) longitudinal measures of pubic hair growth were combined with the assessment of peakheight velocity in the comparison of maturation status constellations (see pp. 82, 97).

Table 15
Relationship between Height and Mental Scores, Boys[a]

			Nonverbal			Verbal				
Grade–age	Socioeconomic group	N	Numerical analogies	Raven	GSAT	Verbal analogies I	Verbal analogies II	Deductive reasoning	Vocabulary	Sentence completion
6 (12)	Upper middle class	41								
	Lower middle class	50			+31*			+31*	+32*	
	Disadvantaged	81–86				+22*				
7 (13)	Upper middle class	32	+38*						+34†	
	Lower middle class	44					+34*			
	Disadvantaged	71–73	+26*	+23*		+28*	+26*		+53†	+35*
	Retarded	18–21	+30			+20				+39
8 (14)	Upper middle class	36	+38*			+35*	+38*		+44*	
	Lower middle class	38								
	Disadvantaged	15–23	+34	+34		+25		+46*		
	Retarded	21–26	+34†	+41*		+48*	+24	+35		

[a]Data are Spearman rank correlation coefficients.

†$p = .1$.
*$p = .05$.

Table 16
Relationship between Growth of Pubic Hair and Mental Development, Boys[a]

			Nonverbal			Verbal				
Grade	Socioeconomic	N	Numerical analogies	Raven	GSAT	Verbal analogies I	Verbal analogies II	Deductive reasoning	Vocabulary	Sentence completion
7 and 8	Upper and lower middle class	35–39	3.8*	2.1	3.3*	1.2	−0.5	0.1	0.6	0.5
7 and 8	Upper middle	20–24	5.1**	3.2	6.6**	2.7	1.1	0.5	1.9	1.3†

[a]Partners with earlier and later pubic hair growth, matched for chronological age. Tabulated data are differences of scores between earlier and later maturing matched partners.

† $p = .1$.
* $p = .05$.
** $p = .01$.

relationship between physical and mental growth which is most pronounced during the pubertal physical growth spurt (ages 13 and 14) in three of the four groups investigated.

When growth of pubic hair was used as a criterion of pubertal maturation in pairs drawn from the middle class sample matched for chronological age, mental differences reflected earlier or later maturation. They are more pronounced in the upper middle class group and definitely larger on two nonverbal tests, numerical analogies and GSAT (p = .02). A significant difference on the verbal analogies test appears only in the upper middle class population (Table 16).

In both disadvantaged groups (study III) the relationship between pubic hair growth and mental tests was assessed by correlational techniques. As can be seen from Table 17, the results confirm the assumption that physiological and mental development are interrelated. There are pronounced relations to nonverbal tests (and to verbal analogies) similar to those found in the middle class sample.

Evidence of an Adolescent Mental Growth Spurt

The demonstration of an adolescent mental growth spurt poses methodological difficulties, chiefly because it cannot be based on measurements of growth increments (as can physical development). Mental score differences over the relatively short period of pubertal growth acceleration cannot be said to form interval scales. The occurrence of a mental growth spurt then can only be inferred from available cross-sectional and longitudinal data.

Among the female samples, relationships between mental achievement and physiological maturation tend to vanish as menarche approaches,* i.e., around the age of 13, the mean menarcheal age in Israel. After menarche (age 14), the relationship tends to invert, the girls maturing later show mental superiority (Table 14). A similar pattern appears in correlations between height and mental scores (Table 13), which tend to become negative at the eighth grade level (age 14), the smaller girl, presumably maturing later, scores higher on mental tests. This could support hypothesis 2 (occurrence of a pubertal mental growth spurt) if the assumption—based on the possibility that late menarche is the result of two different antecedent circumstances—could be substantiated.

Late menarche could be (*a*) the result of generally slower physical and mental development, taking the form of a later start (and consequently a later termination) of the physical and mental growth spurt (see Figure 3, part A) or (*b*) the result of a prolonged growth spurt that starts simultaneously in both those who mature early and those mature late but lasts longer in the latter (see Figure 3, part B). The second situation would lead to taller stature and greater mental

---

*This pattern does not appear to be caused by restriction of range. Similar results were also obtained using matched pairs techniques.

Table 17

Relationship between Growth of Pubic Hair and Mental Development, Boys[a]

Grade–age	Socioeconomic group	N	Nonverbal			Verbal				
			Numerical analogies	Raven	GSAT	Verbal analogies I	Verbal analogies II	Deductive reasoning	Vocabulary	Sentence completion
6 (12)	Disadvantaged	71–79	+27*	+29**						
	Retarded	—								
7 (13)	Disadvantaged	71–73				+20				
	Retarded	19–21	+52*	+48*		+46*	+32	+22	+56*	+41
8 (14)	Disadvantaged	13	+55*	+35		+61*	+27	+40		+40
	Retarded	18–23		+50*		+20		+23	−25	−22

[a] Data are Spearman rank correlation coefficients.

*p = .05.

**p = .01.

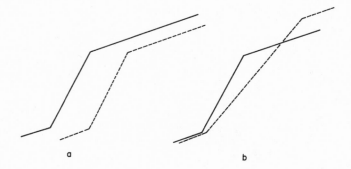

Figure 3 Paradigmatic representation of two types of late maturing subjects (– – –) compared to an early maturing (——) matched partner assuming the occurrence of a mental growth spurt.

achievements among girls who mature late (assuming that a mental growth spurt does occur), for they have the chance to experience intensified physical and mental growth for a longer period. Such a phenomenon would conform to the characteristics of the Sheldonian ectomorphic male, described by Jones (1965) as a type whose pubertal growth spurt is prolonged, whose puberty starts late, and whose mental abilities are superior to the mesomorphic and endomorphic somatypes.

Obviously, type B late maturing subjects would be more frequent in higher age groups where their mental superiority would either neutralize or invert- the relationship between early maturation and mental precocity found in the younger samples. The incidence of type B may be ethnically, culturally, or genetically determined. This would explain the differences in mental and physio-logical maturation between the two socioeconomic groups of female eighth graders. Differentiating two types of late maturers may also throw light on the contrast between the findings of Douglas and Ross and those of Nisbet and Illsley (see p. 78). According to Douglas, Nisbet's sample was biased towards the upper socioeconimic level which was similar to our upper middle class groups.

However, these findings provide no convincing support of hypothesis 2. First, the temporary nature of our study precluded an examination prepubertal and postpubertal differences like those presented by Douglas and Ross (1964) and Nisbet and Illsley (1963), so that mental precocity of subjects maturing earlier might have been found both much earlier and much later than puberty.

Second, the disappearance of the earlier maturers' mental superiority with the approach of puberty could be ascribed not to cessation of the growth spurt but

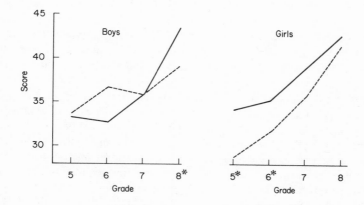

Figure 4 Sex differences in developmental patterns between height and Raven scores in pairs of taller (——) and smaller (– – –) pupils matched by age (upper middle class group only). (* Score difference significant at .05 level.)

to the greater emotional sensitivity and instability of pubertal girls that might temporarily lower their mental achievements.

One rather episodic finding, corroborated from data of study II, might be considered support for hypothesis 2. A comparison of the Raven scores of taller and shorter partners matched by age in the upper middle class sample disclosed the patterns shown in Figure 4. Although the taller girls are mentally superior during fourth, fifth, and sixth grade (in grades 5 and 6, $p = .05$), this trend disappears by eighth grade. Among boys, the pattern is reversed. Only the taller eighth graders have significantly higher Raven scores. These data support hypothesis 2 that mental differences between taller and smaller subjects would appear only during the periods of the adolescent growth spurt. (A similar picture is obtained by plotting achievements on the GSAT.) No such patterns were observed for any test in the lower middle class sample.

Finally, a comparison of the maturational status constellations lends some support to hypothesis 2. (For detailed tabulated data, see Kohen-Raz, 1969.) This comparison could be carried out on only a part of the middle class sample. A reliable location of the growth spurt based on a longitudinal plot of growth curves was not always possible, chiefly because of the relatively short follow-up period.

Among upper middle class girls, significant mental differences in matched pairs of subjects maturing earlier and later appeared when the latter were approaching or undergoing their growth spurts and the former were menarcheal. The differences disappeared when both partners were postmenarcheal. In the lower middle class group, the most pronounced mental differences were found when both partners had passed their physical growth spurts and entered the early post-menarcheal phase. This difference between the two environmental groups would be in line with the findings reported in Table 14 that indicate the persistence of positive relationships between menarcheal age and mental scores in lower middle class (predominantly postmenarcheal) sixth graders.

Upper middle class boys who matured earlier did not attain superiority before they were at stages four or five of pubic hair development and at peak of their growth spurts. At that point, their matched partners were only at the beginning of pubertal growth. These results correspond essentially to the data presented in Table 16. Among lower middle class boys, significant mental differences were found only when the two partners were still in the prepubertal phase, a finding difficult to interpret. This finding is also reflected in the significant correlations between height and mental scores in the prepubertal fifth and sixth graders (see Table 15).

These data roughly suggest that there may be "critical" phases during which physiologically more mature subjects are mentally superior to less developed partners of the same age and socioeconomic background. However, the timing of these phases seems to vary among different socioeconomic groups, a situation that is difficult to explain given our present state of knowledge.

Some of the findings appear to contradict hypothesis 2. In study II, longitudinal data from mental tests of girls were correlated with distance from menarche,* during the premenarcheal, menarcheal, and postmenarcheal phases at two examination dates, one 12 months after the other. If a mental growth spurt had occured (parallel to physiological growth acceleration), after one year correlations within the same population, which had changed from premenarcheal to menarcheal or postmenarcheal, should shrink or disappear. As shown in Table 18, this is not the case. Correlations on mental tests (with the exception of verbal analogies I at grade six) remain fairly stable and even increase in some instances. Correlations with height (bottom row in Table 18) substantially decrease, as would be predicted, confirming that the well-known physical growth spurt does indeed occur, an observation that obviously did not need demonstration by such methods. In favor of hypothesis 2, it might be argued that the mental growth spurt may not coincide with the physical growth spurt and that it may stretch over a longer period than 1 year. To confirm or disprove such an argument, a replication of the investigation, using similar methodology but with larger samples over a longer period would be needed.

Another finding that weakens hypothesis 2 is the fact that in the lower middle

---

Distance from menarche was defined as the number of months between the date of testing and the month of menarche. Since most girls were still premenarcheal at the time of testing, this measure was obtained at the end of the study.

Table 18

Menarcheal Age, Distance from Menarche, Mental Test Scores, and Height, Girls (Entire Middle Class Sample)

| | Grade 6 | | Grade 7 | |
Examination number	I	II	I	II
N	43	43	63	63
Age	11.4	12.4	12.5	13.5
Age at menarche	12.2	12.2	12.11	12.11
Distance from menarche (months)	−10	+2	−6	+6
Spearman rank correlation between menarcheal age, mental scores, and height				
Numerical analogies	−30†	−31†	−04	−15
Raven matrices	−33	−30†	−18	−30
GSAT	−15	−32†	−15	−06
Verbal analogies I	−48**	−32†	+02	+04
Verbal analogies II	−41*	−34†	−03	−01
Deductive reasoning	−43*	−55**	−06	−05
Vocabulary	−27†	−23	+03	−08
Sentence completion	−28	−31†	−08	−03
Height	−21	−06	−36*	−17

$^{†}p = .1.$
$^{*}p = .05.$
$^{**}p = .01.$

class and disadvantaged samples we find pronounced relationships between height and mental scores among preadolescent boys considerably before they begin their growth spurts. The lower middle class girls who mature earlier likewise remain mentally precocious in the postmenarcheal phase.

Some comments should be made about the differential effects of physiological maturation on different mental functions in the two sexes as they emerged in the middle class and disadvantaged samples. Nonverbal reasoning seems to be affected by physical maturation predominantly in boys and only marginally in girls. Verbal test scores, however, are rather strongly influenced by maturation in girls,* but only sporadically in boys. This is in accordance with Ljung's finding of phase differences in the maturation of mathematical and verbal comprehension in boys and girls, indicating that girls have a relatively slow growth rate in mathematics and a more rapid mental maturation in verbal comprehension while the situation is exactly the reverse for boys (1965, p. 248).

In the upper middle class group, visuospatial analogies tested by the Raven and GSA tests are affected by physical maturation in both sexes, with a typical

---

*In this context, Pineau's findings should be cited. He found a positive relationship between birth weight and verbal test performance in prepubertal girls (Pineau, 1970).

difference in timing that corresponds roughly to the timing discrepancy between their physical growth spurts (see Figure 3).

Effects of Experimental Tutoring on Formal Reasoning

Table 19 summarizes experimental effects of the first experimental period upon culturally disadvantaged adolescents after a 6-month training program in tasks of formal reasoning given twice a week for 1 hour (for full details of the method, training schedule, and procedure, see Kohen-Raz, 1973). It can be seen that any experimental effects are weak or absent altogether with the possible exception of those of the seventh grade level which appear a year later at retest. At the eighth grade level, training was absolutely ineffective. These findings, if replicated, would nevertheless suggest that a critical period of susceptibility to training emerges at the seventh grade level. In the case of study III, such findings were not confirmed during the second experimental period on a different sample (Kohen-Raz, 1973), so that at present hypothesis 3 is not supported, although the results justify further investigations of the subject.

Interaction between Experimental Treatment and Physiological Maturation

Only in the sample of female seventh graders were interaction effects between experimental treatment and physiological maturation observed in scores on the numerical analogies and Raven tests (p = .05 and .001 respectively). In that experimental group, girls maturing later were superior to controls who matured earlier. These findings are too sporadic and too isolated to support hypothesis 4 which consequently has to be rejected by the results of study III.

DISCUSSION

To sum up the findings of the three studies, the results generally confirm hypothesis 1 that physiological maturation is related to mental growth in both sexes. The more crucial question of hypothesis 2, whether this physiologically determined mental precocity is linked—exclusively or contributorially—to the pubertal physical growth spurt, does not seem to be unambiguously substantiated.

Hypothesis 3 is very weakly supported by the data, but the findings justify a replication of efforts to train culturally disadvantaged adolescents in higher forms of reasoning. Actually, other studies, described in detail elsewhere, although they were not designed to examine the psychophysiological aspects of these issues, have shown a conspicuous success in stimulating mental growth in these populations (Feinstein and Giovacchini, 1974).

Table 19
Effects of Training in Formal Reasoning on Culturally Disadvantaged Adolescents

Retest number[a]	Grade 6		Grade 7		Grade 8
	I	II	I	II	I
N experimental	34	34	30	31	26
N placebo controls	30	33	30	29	25
N distant controls	83	103	84	76	52
Significance levels of F tests between retest scores of experimental and control groups					
Numerical analogies	.04	NS	.001	.07	NS
Verbal analogies	NS	NS	NS	.02	NS
Raven matrices	NS	NS	NS	NS	NS

[a] Retest II was administered one year after retest I.

Finally, hypothesis 4 must be rejected on the basis of present evidence. Nevertheless, as our studies have shown, physiological maturation is related to mental growth, and the investigation cited (Feinstein *et al.*, 1974) clearly demonstrates training effects. Maturation and learning may not interact but operate independently at different phases of development. Possibly the demonstration of such interaction requires larger samples, more extended and intensive training, a longer longitudinal period of follow up, and more sophisticated techniques of measurement.

The papers by Nisbet and Illsley (1963), Douglas and Ross (1964), Ljung (1965), and the substantiation of hypothesis 1 in our studies lend support to the assumption that mental and physical growth are interrelated and linked somehow to pubertal maturation. The psychophysiological mechanisms responsible for these interactions, however, have not yet been made clear. Interesting material on the relationship between cognitive functions and the differential exposure of the nervous system to adrenergic (ergotropic) and cholinergic (trophotropic) hormonal processes has recently been corroborated by Broverman and Klaiber (1974), Mackenberg, Broverman, and Klaiber (1974), and Broverman, Broverman, Vogel, and Palmer (1964). Comparing morning and afternoon hormonal levels and mental performance in the same subjects, these authors found that overlearned, rather mechanized mental tasks seem to benefit from adrenergic dominance in the morning, but that cholinergic dominance, typically occuring in the afternoon, facilitates perceptual restructuring, field independence, cognitive flexibility, and mental activity requiring distance and contemplation. According to other results obtained in these investigations, persons with a cognitive style characterized by strong automatization have relatively high androgen excretion and early puberty and physiological maturation. Individuals with weak automatizers mature late and are typically tall with "schizotypic" body build (Broverman, Broverman, Vogel, & Palmer, 1964).

It is difficult to see how these data could be used to explain the relationship between physiological maturation and mental growth at adolescence demonstrated in this chapter. It seems, however, that if the survey approach on which our results are based could be supplemented by the stricter experimental methods applied by Broverman and his colleagues, a fruitful approach to this psychophysiological interlinkage could be found.*

To conclude, we recommend that the theoretical and practical aspects of the subject should be separated. Although exploring the linkage between physical and mental growth is of considerable theoretical importance and likely to stimulate interdisciplinary research and lead to interesting discoveries, its *practical* implications, including selection procedures, possible revalidations of testing instruments, educational streaming, segregation of the sexes, and the revision of curricula, must be considered with great caution.

Considering their implications for the field of education of the culturally disadvantaged, the results encourage efforts to develop curricula and methods to foster the development of higher mental functions in these populations. These findings also contradict the widely accepted belief that early mental growth and early environmental impairment in disadvantaged children should be the focus of educational interest. This attitude implicitly deflects attention from the abundant possibilities to stimulate the minds of disadvantaged adolescents at a phase of their development erroneously considered to be too late.

---

*Another approach to the problem has been attempted by investigations on precocious puberty as related to intelligence (Money and Neill, 1967).

9

Concluding Remarks

As stated in the preface, it does not seem possible, given current knowledge, to present a comprehensive theory of the psychobiological aspects of cognitive growth. Nor does this book attempt to survey the vast amount of research concerning the physiological correlates of behavior. This presentation was intended to highlight certain theoretical approaches and empirical findings that might provide the educator, child psychologist, and guidance worker with some new outlooks on certain psychological and educational issues, traditionally considered to be predominantly of a psychosocial nature.

Although the gaps in our knowledge are still wider than the fragments of information we possess, the investigations and considerations described in the preceding chapters permit several theoretical and practical approaches to child development to be reappraised and enriched in both content and methodology.

First, biosemiotic and Piagetian theory suggest the advantage of cybernetic over energetic interpretations of biological and behavioral phenomena. Both theories also draw attention to the contribution of ethological research to the understanding of human development. They actually indicate that we should not only extrapolate the results of laboratory experiments with animals but attempt to undertake comparative analyses of the animals' total behavior and response inventories in coping with genetic pressures and environmental stress throughout their lives and in their natural habitats. Through such comparisons, the differential roles of the various centers and control mechanisms within the central nervous system in cognitive functioning and functional changes in cerebral integration at successive developmental stages can be estimated more clearly. Decisive phases in the child's mental growth thus may turn out to be linked with "integrative shifts" within the central nervous system such as those presumably involved in the evolution of bilateral manipulation and achievement of object constancy in infancy, the improvement of static balance and increase of "movement internalization" at school entrance age, and pubertal alterations of metabolic and hormonal equilibrium possibly linked with the development of higher forms of reasoning.

There is no doubt that the question of "critical phases" in mental development needs to be reexamined. It seems more and more likely that mental growth is not a smooth linear process decelerated or accelerated by cultural deprivation or enrichment but a complex sequence of structural changes determined by "stage specific" interaction with the social and physical environment. In this interaction, the "imitative," "appetitive," and "self-stimulative" activities *initiated* by the child himself seem to play a major role. This capacity for "self-induced" stimulation may be constitutional to some degree, but it is certainly in danger of being severely impaired by adverse environmental circumstances (including intrauterine damage) during "critical phases" of ontogenetic growth.

Another issue emerging from the material presented on birth-season effects, is the "long-term" or "delayed" impact of biological or psychobiological events occuring near the time of birth on mental growth. This calls for a developmental model based on "delayed effects" or "critical timetable setting" complementary to the generally accepted model based on the cumulative effects of early traumatization or overstimulation.

In the light of the findings on the relationship between pubertal physiological maturation and intellectual development, adolescence must be reconsidered as a critical period of mental growth and not, as traditionally described, a period of stabilization and fixation of an intelligence quotient that is almost irreversibly determined by genetic endowment and childhood experiences.

As for more practical implications, it seems that the psychological evaluation of motor development, especially of static balance ability and the versatile use of both hands, should be given a more prominent place in psychodiagnostic batteries used to assess levels and patterns of cognitive abilities. In a similar vein, the measurement of muscle tonicity should be given more serious consideration in the clinical evaluation of mental functions in infancy and in the diagnosis of learning disorders. Given the increasing evidence that metabolic and hormonal processes decisively influence cognitive development, the assessment of their causes and effects may become increasingly important in routine physical examinations of kindergarten and school children.

School entrance age turns out to be a critical period of development, irrespective of the related administrative problems. Psychobiological evaluation of school readiness therefore seems imperative.

With respect to the educational problems of the culturally disadvantaged child, the subtle interaction of minor biological impairments and socioeconomic stress should be considered seriously in the diagnosis of "organic," "familial," or "cultural" retardation (if this distinction is still tenable at all in its traditional form). In any case, it seems unwise to neglect the exploration of psychobiological aspects of cultural disadvantage, simply out of fear that methods and results might encourage "racist" approaches to the problem. This attitude, besides being unscientific in principle, confuses the biological determination of intellectual growth with the prospect of reversing of its potential outcome. There is no justification whatsoever for assuming that an early (genetically or constitutionally induced) mild or moderate central nervous system dysfunction is less curable than a purely psychogenic early traumatization.

Finally, the approaches and methods described in this book may provide a framework for interdisciplinary research and service. Because many of the problems discussed here seem to attract biologists, pediatricians, educators, and child psychologists, interdisciplinary investigations along these lines could lead to fruitful cooperation among these professions focusing on the problems and well-being of normal and exceptional children and adolescents.

References

Abernethy, E. M. Relationship between mental and physical growth. *Monographs of the Society for Research in Child Development,* 1936, *1*(Serial No. 7).

Anastasi, A. *Differential psychology.* New York: Macmillan, 1958.

Armstrong, H. G. A comparison of the performance of summer and autumn born children at 11 and 16. *British Journal of Educational Psychology,* 1966, *36,* 72–76.

Aslin, R. N., & Salapatek, P. Saccadic localisation of visual targets by the very young human infant. *Perception & Psychophysics,* 1975, *17,* 293–302.

Bartlett, F. *Thinking: An experimental study.* London: Allen & Unwin, 1958.

Bates, J. A. V. Electrical activity of the cortex accompanying movement. *Journal of Physiology,* 1951, *113,* 240–257.

Benech, A. Le poids de naissance et ses liasons avec le développement pubertaire chez des garçons de 13 ans. *Biometrie Humaine,* 1970, *5,* 75–78. (a)

Benech, A. Variations saisonnières du poids de naissance. *Biometrie Humaine,* 1970, *5,* 63–74. (b)

Berenberg, S. R. (Ed). *Puberty: biological and psychosocial components.* Proceedings of a conference held under the auspices of Josiah Macy, Jr. Foundation and the International Childrens Center, Paris, December, 1974. Leiden: Stenfert, Kroese, 1975.

Bergmans, J., & Grillner, S. Reciprocal control of spontaneous activity and reflex effects in static and dynamic flexor gamma neurons. *Acta Physiologica Scandinavica,* 1969, *77,* 106–124.

Birch, H. G., & Belmont, L. Auditory-visual integration, intelligence and reading ability in school children. *Perceptual and Motor Skills,* 1965, *20,* 295–305.

Birch, H. G., & Lefford, A. Visual differentiation, intersensory integration, and voluntary motor control. *Monograph of the Society for Research in Child Development,* 1967, *32*(2) Serial No. 110, 1–87.

Bloom, B. *Stability and change in human characteristics.* New York: Wiley, 1964.

Bransford, J. D. Sentence and memory: A constructive vs. interpretive approach. *Cognitive Psychology,* 1972, *3,* 193–209.

Bransford, J. D., & McCarell, N.S. A sketch of a cognitive approach to comprehension. Some thoughts about understanding what it means to comprehend. In W. B. Weimer and D. S. Palermo (Eds.), *Cognition and the symbolic processes.* New York: Wiley, 1974.

Broverman, D. M., Broverman, K., Vogel, W., & Palmer, R. D. The automatization cognitive style and physical development. *Child Development,* 1964, *35,* 1343–1359.

Broverman, D. M., & Klaiber, E. L. Short term vs. long term effects of adrenal hormones on behavior. *Psychological Bulletin,* 1974, *81,* 672–694.

Bruner, J. S., & Koslowski, B. Visual pre-adapted constituents of manipulatory action. *Perception,* 1972, *1,* 1–122.

Bruner, J. S. Pacifier produced visual buffering in human infants. *Developmental Psychobiology,* 1973, *6,* 45–51.

Cattell, R. B. *Personality and motivation.* London: Harrap, 1957.

Connors, C. K. Psychopharmacologic treatment of children. In A. DiMascio & R. Shader (Eds.), *Handbook of psychopharmacology.* New York: Science House, 1970.

Corbin, H. P. F., & Bickford, R. G. Studies of the electroencephalogram of normal children. *Electroencephalography and Clinical Neurophysiology,* 1955, *7,* 15–28.

Craig, W. Appetites and aversions as constituents of instincts. *Biological Bulletin,* 1918, *34,* 91–107.

Cratty, B. J. Perceptual motor behavior and educational progress. Springfield, Ill.: Thomas, 1969.

Cratty, B. J. *The effects of a program of learning games upon selected academic abilities in children with learning difficulties.* Los Angeles: University of California, Department of Education, 1970.

Davies, A. M. Season of birth, intelligence and personality measures. *British Journal of Psychology,* 1964, *55,* 475–476.

Davis, F. B. *The measurement of mental capability through evoked potential recordings.* Greenwich, Conn.: Educational Records Bureau, 1971.

Delacato, C. H. *Neurological organization and reading.* Springfield, Ill.: Thomas, 1966.

Deutsch, M. *The disadvantaged child.* New York: Basic Books, 1967.

Dey, J. D. *Theory and practice governing the time of school entrance.* Edmonton: University of Alberta, 1958.

Dinnage, R. *The handicapped child.* London: Longman and National Children's Bureau, 1970.

Dobzhansky, T. On types, genotypes, and the genetic diversity in population genetics. In J. Spuhler (Ed.), *Genetic diversity and human behavior.* Chicago: Aldine, 1967.

Dobzhansky, T. Evolution of mankind in the light of population genetics. In *Proceedings of the XIIth International Congress of Genetics* (Vol. 3). Tokyo: Science Council of Japan, 1969.

Donaldson, M. *A study of children's thinking.* London: Tavistock, 1963.

Douglas, J. W. B., & Ross, J. M. Age of puberty as related to educational ability, attainment and school leaving age. *Journal of Child Psychology and Psychiatry,* 1964, *5,* 185–196.

Dreyfus-Brisac, C. The bioelectrical development of the central nervous system during early life. In F. Faulkner (Ed.), *Human development.* Philadelphia & London: Saunders, 1966.

Edtfeld, A. W. *Silent speech and silent reading.* Stockholm: Almquist & Wiksell, 1959.

Eibl-Eibesfeldt, I. *Ethology: The biology of behavior.* New York: Holt, Rinehart & Winston, 1970.

Ela, S. *Developmental differences in primary reaching response of young infants from varying social backgrounds.* Unpublished M. A. thesis. Hebrew University, The School of Education, 1973.

Ellingson, R. J. The study of brain electrical activity in infants. In L. P. Lipsitt and C. C. Spiker (Eds)., *Advances in child development and behavior.* Vol. 3. New York: Academic Press, 1967. Pp. 53–97.

Epstein, H. T. Phrenoblysis. Special brain and mind growth periods. Developmental Psychobiology, *1974,* 7, 207–224.

Ertl, J. Evoked potentials, neural efficiency and IQ. In Proctor (Ed.), *Biocybernetics of the central nervous system.* Boston: Little Brown, 1969.

Fantz, R. L. The origin of form perception. *Scientific American,* 1961, *204*(5), 66–88.

Faust, M. S. Developmental maturity as a determinant of prestige of adolescent girls. *Child Development,* 1960, *31,* 173–184.

Feinstein, S. C., & Giovacchini, P. (Ed.). Developmental patterns of higher mental functions in culturally disadvantaged adolescents. In *Annals of Adolescent Psychiatry,* Vol. 3. New York: Basic Books, 1974. Pp. 152–167.

Fischer, A. E. Chemical stimulation of the brain. *Scientific American,* 1964, *210*(6), 60–70.

Fitt, A. B. Seasonal influence on growth function and inheritance. *Educational Research Series* (No. 17). New Zealand Council for Educational Research, Wellington, 1941.

Flament, P. Dévelopment de la preference manuelle de la naissance à six mois. *Enfance,* 1963, May–September, Vol. 3, 241–262.

Frankenstein, C. *The roots of the ego.* Baltimore: Williams & Wilkins, 1966.

Franks, J., & Bransford, J. D. Memory for syntactic form as a function of semantic context. *Journal of Experimental Psychology,* 1974, *103,* 1037–1039.

Franks, J. Towards understanding. In W. B. Weimer & D. S. Palermo (Eds.), *Cognition and the symbolic processes.* New York: Wiley, 1974.

French, I. D. The reticular formation. *Scientific American, 1957,* 196(5), 54–74.

Freud, S. Beyond the pleasure principle. In *Complete works of Sigmund Freud* (Vol. 18). London: Hogarth Press, 1968. (a)

Freud, S. Totem and taboo. In *Complete works of Sigmund Freud* (Vol. 13). London: Hogarth Press, 1968. (b)

Frisch, R. E., & Revelle, R. Height and weight at menarche and a hypothesis of critical body weight and adolescent events. *Science,* 1970, *169,* 397–399.

Fuller, R. Psychological results in treated phenylketonuria. In J. Zubin & G. A. Jervis (Eds.), *Psychopathology of mental development.* New York: Grune & Stratton, 1967.

Gastaut, H. Correlations between the electroencephalic and the psychometric variables. *Electroencephalography and Clinical Neurophysiology,* 1960, *12,* 226–227.

Gazzaniga, M. S., Bogen, J. E., & Sperry, R. W. Dyspraxia following division of the cerebral commissures. *Archives of Neurology,* 1967, *16,* 606–612.

Gesell, A., & Ames, L. B. The development of handedness. *Journal of Genetic Psychology,* 1947, *70,* 155–175.

Giannitrapani, D. EEG average frequency and intelligence. *Electroencephalography and Clinical Neurophysiology,* 1969, *27,* 480–486.

Gibson, J. J. *The senses considered as a perceptual system.* Boston: Houghton Mifflin, 1966.

Gouin-Décarie, T. *Intelligence and affectivity in early childhood.* New York: International University Press, 1965.

Granit, R. The functional role of the muscle spindle's primary end organs. *Proceedings of the Royal Society of Medicine,* 1968, *61,* 69–78.

Gregory, R. L. Seeing as thinking. An active theory of perception. *London Times Literary Supplement,* 707–708. June 23, 1972.

Gregory, R. L. *Eye and brain. The psychology of seeing.* New York: McGraw-Hill, 1966.

Guhl, A. M. The social order of chickens. *Scientific American,* 1956, *194*(2), 42–62.

Guttman, L., & Schlesinger, L. M. *Development of diagnostic analytical and mechanical ability tests through facet design and analysis* (Tech. Rep. U. S. Office of Education Project No. OE–5–21–006). Jerusalem: Israel Institute of Applied Social Research, 1966.

Halpern, L. The syndrome of sensorimotor induction in disturbed equilibrium. *Archives of Neurological Psychiatry*, 1949, *69*, 330–354.

Halpern, L. Additional contribution to the sensorimotor induction syndrome in unilateral equilibrium with special reference to the effect of colors. *Journal of Nervous and Mental Diseases*, 1956, *123*, 334–350.

Halpern, L. Studies on the neurobiological effect of colors. In L. Halpern (Ed.), *Problems of Dynamic Neurology*. Jerusalem: Hebrew University, Hadassa Univ. Hospital, 1963.

Held, R., & Bauer, J. Visually guided reaching in infant monkeys after restricted rearing. *Science*, 1967, *155* (3763), 718–720.

Held, R., Dichgans, J., & Bauer, J. Characteristics of moving visual scences influencing spatial orientation. *Visual Research*, 1975, *15*(3), 357–365.

Held, R. Plasticity in sensori-motor systems. *Scientific American*, 1965, *213*(5), 84–98.

Henry, C. E. Electroencephalograms of normal children. *Monographs of the Society for Research in Child Development*, 1944, *9*(Serial No. 39).

Hetzer, H., & Tent, L. *Der Schulreifetest*. Lindau: Piorkoviski, 1958.

Hinde, R. A., & Steel, E. Integration of the reproductive behavior of female canaries. In *Nervous and hormonal mechanisms of integration* (Symposia of the Society for Experimental Biology, No. 20). Cambridge: Cambridge University Press, 1966.

Hochberg, J. Higher order stimuli and inter-response coupling in the perception of the visual world. In R. B. McLoed and H. L. Pick (Eds.), *Perception: Essays in honor of James J. Gibson*. Ithaca, New York Cornell Univ. Press, 1974.

Hyden, H. Biochemical aspects of learning and memory. In K. H. Pribram (Ed.), *On the biology of learning*. New York: Harcourt, Brace & World, 1969.

Ilg, F. L., & Ames, L. B. *School readiness*. New York: Harper & Row, 1964.

Ilg, F. L., Ames, B. L., & Apell, R. J. School readiness as evaluated by Gesell developmental, visual and projective tests. *Genetic Psychology Monographs*, 1965, *71*, 61–69.

Inhelder, B., & Piaget, J. *The growth of logical thinking from childhood to adolescence*. New York: Basic Books, 1959.

Jackson, B. *Streaming: An education system in miniature*. London: Routledge & Kegan Paul, 1964.

Jacobson, E. Electrophysiology of mental activities. *American Journal of Psychology*, 1932, *44*, 677–694.

Jencks, C. *Inequality*. New York: Basic Books, 1972.

Jensen, A. R. How much can we boost IQ and scholastic achievement? *Harvard Education Review*, 1969, *39*, 1–123.

Jeurissen, A. Mois de naissance et puberté chez les filles. *Biometrie Humaine*, 1970, *5*, 1–16.

Jinks, J. L., & Fulker, D. W., Comparison of the biometrical, genetical, MAVA, and classical approaches to the analysis of human behavior. *Psychological Bulletin*, 1970, *73*, 311–349.

Johansson, B. A. *Criteria of school readiness*. Stockholm: Almquist & Wiksell, 1965.

Jones, H. E. Relationship in physical and mental development. *Review of Educational Research*, 1939, *9*, 91–102.

Jones, H. E., & Conrad, H. S. Mental development in adolescence. In N. B. Henry (Ed.), *The forty-third yearbook, National Society for the Study of Education* (Part I, Adolescence).

Jones, M. C. Psychological correlates of somatic development. *Child Development*, 1965, *36*, 899–911.

Jones, M. C., & Bayley, N. Physical maturing among boys as related to behavior. *Journal of Educational Psychology*, 1950, *41*, 129–148.

Jones, M. C., & Mussen, P. H. Self-conceptions, motivations and interpersonal attitudes of early and late maturing girls. *Child Development*, 1958, *29*, 491–501.

Kahneman, D. Method, findings and theory in studies of visual masking. *Psychological Bulletin*, 1968, *70*, 404–426.

Kanner, L. *Child psychiatry*. Springfield, Illinois: Thomas, 1972.

Karmel, B. Z. Contour effects and pattern performance in infants. *Child Development*, 1974, *45*, 196–199.

Karmel, B. Z., & Hoffman, R. F. Processing of contour information by human infants evidenced by pattern dependent evoked potentials. *Child Development*, 1974, *45*, 39–48.

Karmel, B. Z., & Maisel, E. B. A Neuronal activity model for infant visual attention. In L. B. Cohen & P. Salapatek, (Eds.), *Infant perception: From sensation to cognition*, Vol. 1. New York: Academic Press, 1975.

Kephart, N. C. The slow learner in the classroom. Columbus, Ohio: Merrill, 1971.

Kessen, W., & Herschenson, M. *Ocular orientation in human newborn infants*. Paper presented at the meeting of the American Psychological Association, Philadelphia, August–September, 1963.

Kessen, W. Salapatek, P., & Haith, M. The visual response of the human newborn to linear contour. *Journal of Experimental Child Psychology*, 1972, *13*, 9–20.

Knobloch, H., & Pasamanick, B. Seasonal variation in the birth of the mentally deficient. *American Journal of Public Health*, 1958, *48*, 1201–1208.

Knott, J. R., Friedman, H., & Bardsley, R. Some EEG correlates of intelligence in eight and twelve year old children. *Journal of Experimental Psychology*, 1942, *30*, 380–91.

Kohen-Raz, R. *Intelligenz und Bewegungsvorstellung*. Zurich: Kreutler, 1954.

Kohen-Raz, R. Movement representations and their role in the development of concept formation at early school age. In *Scripta Hierosolymitana: Studies in psychology* (Vol. 14). Jerusalem: Magnes Press, 1965.

Kohen-Raz, R. The ring–cube test: A brief sampling method for assessing primary development of coordinated bilateral grasp responses in infancy. *Perceptual and Motor Skills Monographs*, 1966, *23*(5) 675–688.

Kohen-Raz, R. Scalogram analysis of some developmental sequences of infant behavior as measured by the Bayley scales of mental development. *Genetic Psychology Monographs*, 1967, *76*, 3–21.

Kohen-Raz, R. *Developmental patterns of static balance ability and their relation to cognitive school readiness* (Tech. Rep. U. S. Office of Education Project No. OEC–9–9–149967–017–057CS). Washington, D. C.: U. S. Office of Education, 1969. (a)

Kohen-Raz, R. *Physiological maturation and the development of formal thought at adolescence* (Tech. Rep. U. S. Office of Education Project No. OEC–1–7–071309–4566). Washington, D. C.: U. S. Office of Education, 1969. (b)

Kohen-Raz, R. Developmental patterns of static balance ability and their relation to cognitive school readiness. *Pediatrics*, 1970, *46*, 276–281. (a)

Kohen-Raz, R. *Impairment and training of static balance ability in educationally handicapped children* (Tech. Rep. U. S. Office of Education Project No. OEC–0–70–1263(607). Washington, D. C.: U. S. Office of Education, 1970. (b)

Kohen-Raz, R. *Growth and acquisition of formal reasoning in culturally disadvantaged adolescents as related to physiological maturation*. Dallas, Tex.: Zale Foundation, 1973.

Kohen-Raz, R. Physiological maturation and mental growth at preadolescence and puberty. *Journal of Child Psychology and Psychiatry*, 1974, *15*, 199–213.

Kohen-Raz, R., Russel, A., & Ornoy, A. Early assessment and prevention of socio-cultural deprivation in infancy. *Mental Health and Society*, 1976, *2*, 115–123.

Kohen-Raz, R., & Russel, A. Delayed reaching responses in infants with congenital hip dislocation. In prep.

Köhler, I. The formation and transformation of the perceptual world. *Psychological Issues*, 1964, *3*, No. 4, 1–133.

Kopp, C. B., & Shaperman, J. Cognitive development in the absence of object manipulation during infancy. *Developmental Psychology*, 1973, *9*, 430.

Kreezer, G. L., & Smith, F. W. The relation of the alpha rhythm of the EEG and intelligence level in the nondifferentiated familial type of mental deficiency. *Journal of Psychology*, 1950, *29*, 47–51.

Kuhlen, R. G. The psychology of adolescent development. New York: Harper & Brothers, 1952.

Leiderman, P. *Psychobiological approaches to social behavior*. London: Tavistock Publications, 1965.

Leuba, C., & Friedlander, B. Effects of controlled audio-visual reinforcement on infants manipulative play in the home. *Journal of Experimental Child Psychology*, 1968, *6*, 87–99.

Levine, S. Stimulation in infancy. *Scientific American*, 1960, *202*(5), 80–102.

Liberson, W. T. EEG and intelligence. In J. Zubin & G. A. Jervis (Eds.), *Psychopathology of mental development*. P. 514–543. New York: Grune & Stratton, 1967.

Ljung, B. D. *The adolescent spurt in mental growth*. Uppsala: Almquist, 1965.

Loeser, J. D., & Alvord, E. C. Clinopathological correlations in agenesis of the corpus callosum. *Neurology*, 1968, *18*, 745–756.

Lorenz, K. Comments on the definitions of stages of development. In J. M. Tanner & B. Inhelder (Eds.), *Discussions on child development* (Vol. 4). London: Tavistock Publications, 1960.

Lorenz, K. *Studies in animal and human behavior*. London: Methuen, 1970.

Lunzer, E. A. Problems of formal reasoning in test situations. In P. H. Mussen (Ed.), European research in cognitive development. *Monographs of the Society for Research in Child Development*, 1965, *30*(2), Serial No. 100.

Lunzer, E. A. Formal reasoning. In E. A. Lunzer & J. F. Morris (Eds.), *Development in human learning*. London: Staples Press, 1968.

Luria, A. R. *The working brain*. New York: Basic Books, 1973.

Mackenberg, E. J., Broverman, D. M., Vogel, W., & Klaiber, E. L. Morning to afternoon changes in cognitive performance and in the EEG. *Journal of Educational Psychology*, 1974, *66*, 238–246.

Matheny, A. P., & Dolan, A. B. Persons, situations and time: A genetic view of behavioral change in children. *Journal of Personality & Social Psychology*, 1975, *32*(6), 1106–1110.

McKenzie, B., & Day, R. H. Operant learning of visual pattern discrimination in young infants. *Journal of Experimental Child Psychology*, 1971, *11*, 45–53.

Mead, M. *Male and female*. London: V. Gollancz, 1949.

Meinert, R. Schulreife und Entwicklung. In *Zum Problem der Schulreife*. Beiheft 2 der Zeitschrift Schule und Psychologie. Basel: 1955.

Mills, C. A. Mental and physical development as influenced by season of conception. *Human Biology*, 1941, *13*, 378–389.

Milner, E. *Human neural and behavioral development*. Springfield, Ill.: Thomas, 1967.

Mittler, P. *The study of twins*. Harmondsworth, Middlesex: Penguin Books, 1971.

Moltz, H. Imprinting. *Psychological Bulletin*, 1960, *57*, 291–314.

Money, J., & Neill, J. Precocious puberty, IQ and school acceleration. *Clinical Pediatrics,* 1967, *6*(5), 277–280.

Mundy-Castle, A. C. Electrophysiological correlates of intelligence. *Journal of Personality,* 1958, *26*, 184–199.

Natan, M. *Sources of differences in some abilities of twins as compared to singletons* (in Hebrew). Unpublished M. A. thesis, Hebrew University, Department of Psychology, 1970.

Nisbet, J. D., & Illsley, R. The influence of early puberty on test performance at the age of eleven. *British Journal of Educational Psychology,* 1963, *33*, 176–196.

Nisbet, J. D., Illsley, R., Sutherland, A. E., & Douse, M. J. Puberty and test performance. *British Journal of Educational Psychology,* 1964, *34*, 202–203.

Olds, J. Pleasure centers in the brain. *Scientific American,* 1956, *195*(4), 105–118.

Orme, J. E. Intelligence, season of birth and climatic temperature. *British Journal of Psychology,* 1963, *54*, 273–276.

Ortar, G., & Murieli, A. *MILTA, A group intelligence test for grades 4–12.* Jerusalem: Hebrew University, School of Education, 1965.

Ozer, M. N. The neurological evaluation of school-age children. *Journal of Learning Disabilities,* 1968, *1*, 87–89.

Ozer, M. N., & Deem, M. A. *A standardized neurological examination: Its validity in predicting school achievement* (Final Rep. Contract No. 2389). Washington, D.C.: Office of Economic Opportunities, 1968.

Paine, R. S., & Oppé, T. E. *Neurological examination of children* (Clinics in Developmental Medicine 20–21). London: Spastics International Publications & Heinemann, 1966.

Palàgyi, M. *Wahrnehmungslehre.* Leipzig: Barth, 1925.

Pampiglione, G. Some aspects of development of cerebral function in mammals. *Proceedings of the Royal Society of Medicine,* 1971, *64*, 429–435.

Pampiglione, G., & Quibell, E. P. EEG studies in so-called thalidomide babies. *Electroencephalography and Clinical Neurophysiology,* 1966, *21*, 201–202.

Pasamanick, B., Knobloch, H., & Lilienfeld, A. Socio-economic status and some precursors of neuropsychiatric disorder. *American Journal of Orthopsychiatry,* 1956, *26*, 594–601. 298–305.

Penfield, W. Consciousness, memory, and man's conditioned reflexes. In K. H. Pribram (Ed.), *On the biology of learning.* New York: Harcourt, 1969.

Piaget, J. Le problème neurologique de l'intériorisation des actions en opérations reversibles. *Archives de Psychologie* (Geneva), 1947–1949, *32*, 241–258.

Piaget, J. Principal factors determining intellectual evolution from childhood to adult life. In D. Rapaport, (Ed.), *Organization and pathology of thought.* New York: Columbia University Press, 1951.

Piaget, J. *Psychology of intelligence* London: Routledge & Kegan Paul, 1951.

Piaget, J. *The origin of intelligence in children.* New York: International University Press, 1953.

Piaget, J. *The construction of reality in the child.* New York: Basic Books, 1954.

Piaget, J. *Biologie et connaissance.* Paris: Gallimard, 1967.

Piaget, J. *Biology and knowledge.* Chicago: University of Chicago Press, 1971.

Pineau, M. Poids de naissance. Variations saisonnières chez les filles agées 13 ans. *Biometrie Humaine,* 1970, *5*, 47–62.

Pintner, R., & Forlano, G. Season of birth and intelligence. *Journal of Genetic Psychology,* 1939, *54*, 353–358.

Pintner, R., & Forlano, G. Season of birth and mental differences. *Psychological Bulletin,* 1943, *40*, 25–35.

Prechtl, H., & Touwen, B. C. *The neurological examination of the child with minor nervous dysfunction.* London: Heinemann, 1970.

Pribram, K. H. The four R's of remembering. In K. H. Pribram (Ed.), *On the biology of learning.* New York: Harcourt, Brace & World, 1969.

Pringle, M. L. K. *The challenge of thalidomide.* London: Longman, 1970.

Pritchard, R. M. Stabilized images on the retina. *Scientific American*, 1961, *204*(6) 72–92.

Rapaport, D. *Organization and pathology of thought.* New York: Columbia University Press, 1951.

Rapaport, J. A case of congenital sensory neuropathy diagnosed in infancy. *Journal of Child Psychology and Psychiatry*, 1969, *10*, 63–68.

Raven, J. C. *Progressive matrices.* London: Lewis, 1962.

Rey, A. *Étude des Insuffisiances Psychologique.* Neuchâtel: Delacheaux & Nestlé, 1947.

Rey, A. L'évolution du comportement interne dans la représentation du movement. *Archives de Psychologie* (Geneva), 1947–1949, *32*, 209–234.

Rey, A. *Monographies de psychologie clinique.* Neuchâtel, Delacheau & Nestlé, 1952.

Rey, A. Motricité-intériorisé et dévelopment mental. In *Problèmes du dévelopment mental.* Neuchâtel Delacheaux & Nestlé, 1969.

Rothschild, F. S. *Das Zentralnervensystem als Symbol des Erlebens.* Bibliotheca Psychiatrica et Neurologica, Fasc. 103. Basel & New York: S. Karger, 1958.

Rothschild, F. S. Transzendentale Phänomenologie als Semantik der Strukturen mit psychophysischer Funktion. *Philosophia Naturalis,* 1961, *6*, 485–515.

Rothschild, F. S. Laws of symbolic mediation in the dynamics of self and personality. *Annals of the New York Academy of Science,* 1962, 774–784.

Rothschild, F. S. Posture and psyche. In L. Halpern (Ed.), *Problems of dynamic neurology.* Jerusalem: Hadassah Medical School, 1963.

Rutter, M., Graham, P., & Yule, W. *A neuropsychiatric study in childhood* (Clinics in Developmental Medicine 35–36). London: Heinemann, 1970.

Sainsburg, H. The relationship of the season of birth to the state of primary dentition. *Journal of Dental Research,* 1965, *35*, 909–913.

Salapatek, P., & Kessen, W. Visual scanning of triangles by the human newborn. *Journal of Experimental Child Psychology,* 1966, *3*, 115–167.

Salapatek, P. Visual scanning of geometrical figures by the human newborn. *Journal of Comparative and Physiological Psychology,* 1968, *66*, 247–258.

Salapatek, P. & Kessen, W. Prolonged investigation of a plane geometric triangle by the human newborn. *Journal of Experimental Child Psychology,* 1973, *15*, 22–39.

Sarason, S. B. *Psychological problems in mental deficiency.* New York: Harper & Brothers, 1959.

Sargent, F. A critique of homeostasis. Season and metabolism. *Archiv für Meteorologie, Geophysik, and Bioklimatologie* (Series A), 1951, *3*, 242–253.

Scarr-Salapatek, S. Social introversion–extraversion as a heritable response. *Child Development,* 1969, *40*, 823–832.

Scarr-Salapatek, S. An evolutionary perspective on infant intelligence. In M. Lewis (Ed.), *Infant intelligence.* New York: Plenum, 1976.

Senden, M. V. *Space and sight.* New York: Free Press, 1960.

Shaw, R., McIntyre, M., & Mace, W. The role of symmetry in event perception. In R. B. McLoed & H. L. Pick (Eds.), *Perception: Essays in honor of James J. Gibson.* Ithaca: Cornell Univ. Press, 1974.

Shaw, R., & McIntyre, M. Algoristic foundations to cognitive psychology. In W. B. Weimer & D. S. Palermo (Eds.), *Cognition and the symbolic processes,* New York: Wiley, 1974.

Siegel, S. *Non-parametric statistics for the behavioral sciences. New York: McGraw-Hill,* 1965.

Siipola, A., & Taylor, F. Reactions to inkblots under fear and pressure. *Journal of Personality*, 1952, *21*, 22–47.

Skeels, H. M., & Harms, I. Children with inferior social histories: Their mental development in adoptive homes. *Journal of Genetic Psychology*, 1948, *72*, 283–294.

Skodak, M., & Skeels, H. M. A final follow–up study of one hundred adopted children. *Journal of Genetic Psychology*, 1949, *75*, 85–125.

Sloan, W. The Lincoln-Oseretzky motor development scale. *Genetic Psychology Monographs*, 1955, *51*, 183–262.

Sperry, R. W. The great cerebral commissures. *Scientific American*, 1964, *210*(1), 42–63.

Sperry, R. W. Hemisphere deconnection and unity in conscious awareness. *American Psychologist*, 1968, *23*, 723–733.

Sperry, R. W., & Gazzaniga, M. S. Language following surgical disconnection of the hemispheres. In *Brain mechanisms underlying speech and language*. New York: Grune & Stratton, 1967.

Staats, A. W. Intelligence, biology and learning. In H. C. Haywood (Ed.), *Social-cultural aspects of mental retardation* (Proceedings of the Peabody-NIMH Conference). New York: Appleton Century Crofts, 1970.

Stolz, H. R. *Somatic development of adolescent boys.* New York: Macmillan, 1951.

Sutton, P. The correlation between streaming and season of birth in secondary schools. *British Journal of Educational Psychology*, 1967, *37*, 300–304.

Tanner, J. M. *Growth at adolescence.* Springfield, Ill.: Thomas, 1962.

Terman, L. M., & Merrill, M. A. *Measuring intelligence.* Boston: Houghton Mifflin, 1937.

Thurstone, L. L., & Ackerson, L. The mental growth curve for Binet tests. *Journal of Educational Psychology*, 1929, *20*, 569–583.

Tinbergen, N. *The study of instinct.* Oxford: Clarendon, 1955.

Turvey, M. T. On peripheral and central processes in vision. *Psychological Review*, 1973, *80*, 1–50.

Turvey, M. T. Constructive theory, perceptual systems, and tacit knowledge. In W. B. Weimer & D. S. Palermo (Eds.), *Cognition and the symbolic processes*. New York: Wiley, 1974.

Uexküll, J. *Theoretische Biologie.* Berlin: Springer, 1926.

Vande Voort, L., Senf, G. M., & Benton, A. L. Development of audio-visual integration in normal and retarded readers. *Child Development*, 1972, *43*, 1269–1272.

Vogel, W., & Broverman, D. M. EEG and mental abilities. *EEG and Clinical Neurophysiology*, 1968, *24*, 166–175.

Von Holst, E., & Von Saint Paul, U. Electrically controlled behavior. *Scientific American*, 1962, *206*(3) 50–60.

Wallace, B. Pre-exposure pointing frequency effects on adaptation to prismatic viewing. *Perception & Psychophysics*, 1974, *15*, 26–30.

Wallace, B. Target and arm observation effects on adaptation to prism displacement, *Perception & Psychophysics*, 1974, *15*, 145–148.

Wapner, S., & Werner, H. *Perceptual development.* Worcester, Massachusetts: Clark University Press, 1957.

Wehrung, D. A., & Hay, S. The study of seasonal incidence of congenital malformations in the U. S. *British Journal of Preventive Social Medicine*, 1970, *24*, 24–32.

White, B. L., Castle, P., & Held, R. Observations on the development of visually-directed reaching. *Child Development*, 1964, *35*, 349–364.

White, B. L., & Held, R. Plasticity of sensori-motor development in human infants. In J. F. Rosenblith & W. Allensmith (Eds.), *Causes of behavior*. Boston: Allyn and Bacon, 1966.

Wiener, G. The relationship of birth weight and length of gestation to intellectual development at ages 8–10. *Journal of Pediatrics*, 1970, *76*, 694–699.

Willerman, L. Biosocial influence on human development. *American Journal of Orthopsychiatry,* 1972, *42,* 452–462.

Wilson, R. S. Twins: Early mental development.*Science,* 1972, *175,* 914–917.

Wilson, R. S. Twins: Mental development in the preschool years. *Developmental Psychology,* 1974, *10,* 580–588.

Wilson, R. S. Twins: Patterns of cognitive development as measured on the WIPPSI. *Developmental Psychology,* 1975, *11*(2), 126–134.

Wilson, R. S., & Harping, E. B. Mental and motor development in infant twins. *Developmental Psychology,* 1972, 7, 277 287.

Wilson, R. S. Sensori-motor and cognitive development. Paper read at the Conference on Early Behavioral Assessment. Seattle, Washington, 1976.

Woodward, M. The behavior of idiots interpreted by Piaget's theory of sensori-motor development. *British Journal of Educational Psychology,* 1959, *29,* 60–71.

Woodward, M., & Stern, D. J. Developmental patterns of severely subnormal children. *British Journal of Educational Psychology,* 1963, *33,* 10–21.

Zamenhof, S., Marthens, E. van, & Bursztyn, H. The effect of hormones on DNA synthesis and cell number in the developing chick and rat brain. In M. Hamburg & E. J. W. Barrington, *Hormones and development.* New York: Appleton Century Crofts, 1971.

Zeller, W. *Konstitution und Entwicklung.* Göttingen: Verlag Psychologische Rundschau, 1952.

Author Index

Subject Index

Accommodation, 15, 21
Adaptation, 15, 16, 19
Adrenergic hormonal processes, 101
Affective tension, 29
Afference, tactile, 50
Affordance, 34
Age–grade ceiling effect, 72
Agenesis, 47
Aiguillages, 63
Alertness 37
Animal brain, seasonal effects on growth, 75
Anticipatory responses, 17
Anthropometric measures, 56, 57
Appetence, 37
Assimilation, 15, 19, 21
Ataxiametry, 60, 65
Auditory distractibility, 57
Autism (infantile), 9
Automatization, as cognitive style, 101

B

Basic trust, 48
Bayley Scales, 53
Behaviorism, 1, 15
Behavior disturbances, 13
Bender–Gestalt test, 61
Biogenetics, 75
Bilaterality, 46
Bimanual activity (in infants), 46

Bimanual coordination, 47
Bimanual manipulation, 104
Bimanual reaching, 48, 51
Biochemical approaches, 12, 13
Biometric methods, 5
Biosemiotic theory, 11, 12, 31–41, 60, 63
Biosocial etiology, 87
Birth control, 74
    season effect, 51, 67–76
    weight, 72
Blindness, 49, 53
Blind operated subjects, 38
Body tilt, 28, 29
Body–mind interaction, 2, 3
Brain
    injury, 4, 29
    maturation, 77
    organization, 4, 5, 12
    stimulation, 3, 4
British school
    entrance system, 70
    streaming system, 70

C

Canalization, 7
Cataract, 38
Central nervous system, *see* Nervous system
Cerebellum, 35, 38

Organismic tension, 25
Oseretski scales, 63
Ozer's neurological evaluation, 56–59

P

Parental figures, 55
Pediatric diagnosis, 52
Peabody Picture Vocabulary, 57
Perception
  generative, 34, 35
  of invariant structures, 34
  involving masking, 34
  primary, 44
Perceptual deficits, 43
Perceptual development, 11, 25
Perceptual processes, 34
Perceptual responses, 16
Perceptual skills, 16
Peripheral nervous system, 32
Phenomenological approaches, 31, 32, 33
Phenotype, 20
Phenylketonuria, 5, 12, 13, 51
Phyletic level, 33
Phyletic scale, 16, 32
Phylogenic differentiation, 49
Phylogeny, 12
Physical handicap, 51, 52
Physical training, 41
Position sense, 57
Posture, 12, 46
Postural adjustment, 13, 29, 35
Postural equilibrium, 29
Postural system, 35
Pregnancy, 75
Prenatal development, 87
Preoperational reasoning, 22
Primary love object, 48
Primary processes, 27
Prisms, prismatic distortion, 38, 39
Proprioception, 48, 65
Physical training, 41
Physiological psychology, 2
  puberty, 77–101
Psychoanalysis, 2, 19
Psychophysical parallelism, 10
Psychophysics, 1
Puberty, 12, 77ff
Pubertal growth spurt, 77
Pubertal maturation, 77–101

Pubic hair
  development, 82
  examinations, 81
  growth as related to mental development, 91–93

R

Racial determinism, 6
Racist approaches, 105
Raven Matrices, 68, 70, 82, 87, 89, 97
Reaching response (in infants), 45
  top level reach, 45, 46
Reading skill
  ability, 29, 60–62
  readiness, 57, 60–62
  silent, 64
Reafference, 38, 39
Reality
  adaptation, 38
  control, 35
Reasoning
  concrete operational, 55
  formal, 16, 17, 24, 49, 81
Referents (of speech), 48
Releasing schemata, 44
Response
  hierarchies, 9
  inventories, 8, 9, 16
  readiness, 16
Retardation, see Mental retardation
Retarded disadvantaged pupils, 81, 84
Retina, 8
Retinal image, 38
Retinal stimulation, 44
Reticular formation, 33
Reversibility, 17

S

Scalogram, 62, 69, 45
Scanning, see Visual scanning
Schema (developmental), 9
Schizotymic body build, 102
School entrance, 56
  compulsory age, 70, 79
  schedules, 70, 74
School readiness, 55–65
  anthropometric criteria of, 56, 57
  tests, 55

W

Wechsler scales, 7, 72
Weight
    assessment at puberty, 81

critical at menarche, 87
of disadvantaged adolescents, 84–86
seasonal effects on, 71
Weisman's theory, 19
WIPPSI, 7